Praise for *Understanding Serenity*

"You could take away every book I have but one, the one you are now reading, and I could still maintain my own emotional health and love of life."
——Merrill Bailey, M.ED. (from the foreword)

"I was introduced to From *Here to Serenity* while I was going through a very dark period and I'll be the first person to stand up and say this book CHANGED MY LIFE!!! The four principals in the book taught me how to overcome obstacles more than ANY OTHER self help book I've ever read. I feel TOTAL PEACE and for the first time in my life I am truly happy! I would, have, and will CONTINUE to recommend this book to everyone! Jane Nelsen is an amazing author and she has the ability to reach people on many different levels!"
——Wendy Espinoza, West Jordan, Utah

"The reason I recommend *Understanding Serenity* so highly to all of my friends and students is that it give us effective tools for staying on course toward real joy in our lives."
——Max Skousen, my teacher, my friend, (1921-2004)

"I admire your great knowledge and your ability to write from your heart. Your book is amazing, JUST LOVE IT!"
——Blanka Williams

"I recently bought From *Here to Serenity* while on a business trip. I am a student of the *Course in Miracles* and your book is so in tune with the *Course* and has totally clarified for me the head and heart issues that I was not seeing very clearly. I have purple post-its on the pages of this book for sooo many things. It's become so important for my spiritual growth that I refer to the *Feelings Compass Chart* daily and have added some of *my own words* to each of the columns.

I bought the book on a whim, never dreaming that it would relate so closely with the Course. It has made some profound changes in my perceptions already (like every single day I *see* things differently) and this book will definitely be an important one in my spiritual growth and in my life."

—Murielle McEvoy, Ventura, CA

"This is a warm and wonderfully written book which will help people find understanding and compassion in their relationships with children, spouses, friends—and most importantly, themselves."

—Kimberly Kiddo, Psychologist, Coral Gables, FL

"Reading *Understanding* has assisted many of my patients to access that transcendent intelligence from which insight and wisdom emanate. With humility, clarity, and joy, Dr. Nelsen points to this potential within all of us."

—William F. Pettit, M.D., board-certified psychiatrist, West Virginia Initiative for Innate Health, University of West Virginia, Morgantown, WV

"Please send more copies of your wonderful, practical, enlightened, and enlightening book. I just loaned my last one out and don't mind admitting to a little 'separation anxiety.' I like to have a few on hand as 'loaners' to clients."

—Roz Cohen, RN, BC, MSN, Captain Cook Hawaii

"Eric Berne once said there are only three words necessary for living, 'Yes,' 'No,' and 'Wow!' This delightful book is about the 'Wow!' Just let go, trust, and allow the peace of mind to come from within. The truth that sets us free really can be that simple. Jane Nelsen has written of this natural process, which is inherent within all of us, in such an understandable manner. A terrific book to carry around with you."

—Bill Hutcherson, Ph.D. Psychologist, Roseville, CA

"I want to thank you for the insights you provide in your incredible book, *Understanding*. I am trying to apply the principles you teach in every aspect of my life right now. I feel like I need to carry it around with me constantly to remind myself not to listen to my crazy thoughts, but to my heart instead."

—Barbara, Salt Lake City

To my seven children, Teryl, Jim, Ken, Brad, Lisa, Mark, and Mary

I feel so blessed to have you in my life.

Understanding Serenity

What Thoughts are you Giving up Your Happiness For?

Jane Nelsen, Ed.D

Empowering People Books, Tapes, and Videos
www.empoweringpeople.com
1-800-456-7770

Order information

For printed books please visit
http://www.empoweringpeople.com

For e-books please visit
http://www.focusingonsolutions.com

To order product by phone please call
1-800-456-7770

Jane Nelsen is available for lectures and
workshops.
E-mail jane@positivediscipline.com

Contents

Foreword

by Merrill J. Bailey

It is not an exaggeration to say that this book changed my life and, consequently, the lives of literally hundreds of my clients and students over the last several years. When I first was introduced to this book, I had been teaching and counseling for many years. I believed that I was a successful therapist when I helped my clients "cope" with their problems. After all, I was pretty good at "coping" myself.

The first edition, which was titled, *Understanding*, threw me into my heart, where my own healing continued like I would never have imagined possible. I have found this to be true for many of the people I have counseled and taught since that time. I have suggested to my clients that one can't read this work just once or twice. It is a lifetime process of struggling to stay in the heart. This book, written for the layman, takes me back into my *heart* every time I read it. I have reviewed this revision several times and can say with complete honesty that it is better than ever in achieving this end.

The science of the *Psychology of Mind* evolved out of the 1980s. The followers seemed to be a strange mix of mystics and board-certified psychologists. After thoroughly digesting Dr. Nelsen's book, my enthusiasm and personal results from her work drove me to send for and study in depth all of the material I could get my hands on that explained this new science. I soon discovered that there is nothing out there for the ordinary person that comes close to explaining the principles and precepts of this remarkable science as does *Understanding Serenity*.

We seem to have an imbalance leaning toward the "head" in our culture, which makes it very difficult to find lasting joy and satisfaction in all of our relationships. The programmed thought system generates our mental, and most of our physical, ills. It is not easy for those of us who were raised in our thought-dominated culture to grasp the concept of being able to stand back objectively and view how the brain works.

"Not able to see the forest for the trees" is more than just a cliché when it comes to trying to understand ourselves and why we *think* and thus act the way we do. *Understanding Serenity*, in my experience, helps create this new awareness as nothing else in literature is able to do.

I have found that understanding my dysfunction in relationships is, however, only part of the healing equation. There are many practitioners and hoards of books on the market right now that do a wonderful job of helping us see where our emotional problems come from. I agree with Dr. Nelsen that some of this information can be extremely helpful. These excellent works can open the doors for personal growth when used to help people heal old beliefs from the past that block them from accessing their hearts, their inner wisdom, their spiritual source. However, after years of experience, I have found that for a complete life change—a rebirth, if you will—to take place in a person's life, something more than just getting in touch with the reasons for their dysfunction needs to occur. This is where the principles taught in *Understanding Serenity* have had such great impact.

In clear, precise, understandable dialogue, Dr. Nelsen is able to make it easy to get out of the thought system, which creates all dysfunction, and into the heart, where real emotional and behavioral change can begin to take place. Rereading the chapters creates this change effortlessly, even as I read.

Especially helpful are the latter chapters, which contain clear, realistic life experience examples where changing the heart can change the outcomes of previous relationship breakdowns. It seems that emotions are some of the most misunderstood and feared of all constructs within the field of psychology. Understanding that emotions are created instantaneously from feelings and learning that I have control over my feelings is one of the greatest breakthroughs in the study of "mind" in the twentieth century. My feelings are totally different when I am in my heart than when I am in my programmed thought system.

A well-known actor once stated publicly that self-help books had changed his life and that he lived on a steady diet of them. I can personally understand why he could make such a remark. People who are seeking to grow and who are willing to pay the price for that growth will eventually find the way. However, as I have often told my seminar students, you could take away every book I have but one, the one you are now reading, and I could still maintain my own emotional health and love of life. I share with them the honest fact that the equation for personal happiness and contentment in my own life shifted dramatically from a twenty percent happy/eighty percent coping state to a realistic ninety percent happy/ten percent coping state, simply from being introduced to her book many years ago.

Someone said once, "If we continue to do what we've always done, we'll always get what we've always got." Our culture has always enthroned the head or intellect as our master and doggedly insisted on trying to solve all of our problems from that source, not realizing "that source" is the problem. My great hope and dream for the future of mental health in our world is that with renewed *Understanding* we can do something different and thus start reaping better emotional reward—in other words, "change our hearts." This book is more than just a start; it is the very "way."

Introduction and Acknowledgments

This book was first self-published under the title *Understanding: Eliminating Stress and Dissatisfaction in Life and Relationships.* I was totally surprised that so many copies (30,000) sold as a self-published book. The sales were due, in part, to the word-of-mouth popularity among recovery organizations in Minneapolis. For this reason, when Prima Publishing published the book, the title was changed to *Understanding: Eliminating Stress and Finding Serenity in Life and Relationships.* Of course, the sales were much greater with the help of Prima. Later, Prima thought a "better" title might boost sales even more. Thus the change to *From Here to Serenity: Four Principles for Understanding Who You Really Are.* The title change didn't work and sales diminished instead of increasing. When Prima was sold to Random House, they decided not to continue printing this book.

Since *Understanding Serenity* (the title I have chosen for this revision) is my favorite book of the 18 I have authored or co-authored, I want to continue to share it with others. I have now come full circle—back to self-publishing. *Understanding Serenity* is the book that has had the greatest impact on my life and, according to reports I have heard, on the lives of others. Every time I read this book myself, I go to even deeper levels of serenity and listening to my heart.

Introduction to the first editions:

I enjoy personal growth workshops. However, I used to wonder, in jest, if I would ever find the last workshop—one that would finally teach me the magic techniques that would give me enough competence and confidence to be truly helpful to myself and others. I never found what I was looking for. Instead, I found something better—principles that taught me where competence, confidence, and wisdom are and always have been—within myself. I had read and heard, over and over, the advice to go within; but I didn't know how to do it. The intellectual knowledge that *"the kingdom of heaven is within*: and *"as a man thinketh, so is he"* were not new to me, but I had never experienced these truths. I finally discovered a seminar where principles were explained that led me to experience my inner kingdom of happiness and peace of mind. I gratefully acknowledge and give thanks to George Pransky and Robert Kausen, who put up with my "what ifs" and "yes, buts" until finally I was able to hear at a deeper level.

After experiencing such dramatic results in my life, I felt inspired to spend six months in fellowship at the Advanced Human Studies Institute in Coral Gables, Florida. Studying and working with Dr. Rick Suarez and Dr. Kimberly Kiddoo was truly a beautiful and enriching experience. What a privilege it was to be led to a deeper *understanding* of inner resources via the wisdom of these pioneers and innovators of the *Psychology of Mind*.

Introduction and Acknowledgments

It is with loving appreciation that I acknowledge Dr. William Pettit, a prominent psychiatrist who dropped his successful practice and position as a national trainer of a popular personal growth seminar when he heard the principles of *Psychology of Mind*. He moved his family to Florida and was finishing his fellowship at the Advanced Human Studies Institute while I was there. His delightful influence is reflected in this book.

It was a special thrill to receive an endorsement from Wayne Dyer. His books and tapes have been an inspiration to me and my family for years. Wayne continues to inspire me with his spiritual teachings through his new books and lectures on PBS Television.

It has been a gratifying and humbling experience to hear from so many people who have read the first editions of this book. That so many would be touched was beyond my comprehension, and I hope that many more will find joy and serenity through this revised edition.

One reason for the previous revisions was the discovery of additional concepts that deepened my level of understanding. Thanks to Valerie Seeman Moreton and Max Skousen, it now seems like common sense to understand that sometimes we need to heal the beliefs we created as part of our thought systems. Too often these beliefs filter our life experience even when we are not consciously aware of them. Healing is effective and powerful when it is based on an understanding of the four principles discussed in this book.

My good friend, Dr. Bill Hutcherson, has been my workshop buddy for years. We no longer to enjoy the workshops that give validity to the thought system but treasure workshops that take us to our hearts and spiritual sources. Bill offered to read the manuscript for this edition and was very gentle with his suggestions.

Introduction and Acknowledgments

I am especially grateful to my husband, Barry. He is one of the most unconditionally loving people I know. Through *understanding* we have learned to be kind to each other (most of the time), even when we get into the insanity of our programmed thought systems—until the insanity passes.

I don't want to give the impression that life is always total bliss. We are on this planet to learn and to grow. Every experience gives us opportunities for learning and growing at whatever depth we choose. All the principles discussed in *Understanding Serenity* have helped me view both "good" and "bad" experiences with gratitude—sooner or later. You will understand why after reading this book.

My next acknowledgment is to my children, to whom this book is dedicated. We continually love and learn from one another. My daughter Mary made a statement that sums up the value of the principles discussed in this book. I got lost for a short time in feelings of insecurity and was behaving irrationally. Because of my *understanding* of the four principles, it didn't last too long. Mary later said, "I knew you would soon realize what you were doing, Mama."

It is my hope that *Understanding Serenity* will help you *understand* what you are doing, learn from it, and quickly return to your heart, where you will experience joy and serenity.

1

Listening Softly

L ove, happiness, gratitude, wisdom, compassion, serenity.
joy. These are the natural good feelings inherent in every
human being. They are the essence of who you are—your
natural state of mind—your soul. Your soul has no fear, no anger,
no anxiety, and is totally non-judgmental.

Since this is true, why do so many people live in stress,
anxiety, anger, judgment, depression, or fear? Why are so many
searching for happiness through relationships, work, money, more,
better, different? Why do they keep looking outside themselves
when they have heard, over and over, that happiness lies within?

The answer to these questions can be found through the *understanding* that we have all created a thought system that keeps us from experiencing our inherent, natural state of being. Many of us have unwittingly allowed our thought systems to become so powerful that we seldom access the wisdom of our hearts and souls. Listening softly may help you bypass your thought system so you can hear messages from your heart—your ultimate barometer of truth.

In our society, we have been taught to pay more attention to the logic of our intellects than to the joy and wisdom of our hearts. Deepak Chopra suggests another possibility in his book *The Seven Spiritual Laws of Success:*

> *Only the heart knows the correct answer. Most people think the heart is mush and sentimental. But it's not. The heart is intuitive; it's holistic, it's contextual, it's relational. It doesn't have a win-lose orientation. It taps into the cosmic computer—the field of pure potentiality, pure knowledge, and infinite organizing power—and takes everything into account. At times it may not even seem rational, but the heart has a computing ability that is far more accurate and far more precise than anything within the limits of rational thought.[1]*

The brain has unlimited capacity and capabilities. However, we have limited our brains with a thought system *programmed*

---

[1] Deepak Chopra, *The Seven Laws of Spiritual Success* (San Rafael: Amber-Allen Publishing & New World Library, 1994), pp. 43-44.

with old decisions, based on mistaken interpretations that became solid beliefs, which were then seen as reality. This programmed thought system filters out any new possibilities, including the truth; it tries to fit everything into what it already knows—even when that *knowing* is based on illusions. David R. Hawkins, in his book, *Power Vs Force*,[2] describes it this way:

> *"To transcend the limitations of the mind, it's necessary to dethrone it from its tyranny as sole arbiter of reality. The vain mind confers its imprint of authenticity on the movie of life it happens to be viewing; the mind's very nature is to convince us that its unique view of experience is the genuine article. Each individual secretly feels that his particular experience of the world is accurate."*

The concept of separate realities, and the problems we encounter when we really do believe our view of the world is *right*, is explored more thoroughly in Chapter 6.

Throughout this book, *understanding* is italicized to convey a level of inspiration or insight that comes from your inner wisdom, your heart, your soul. You will experience unlimited potentiality when you *understand* that your inner wisdom is *connected* to and *aligns* with *Universal Consciousness* and Wisdom. You will learn how to stop allowing your thought system to create barriers that keep you from such unlimited power and possibility.

---

[2] David R. Hawkins, *Power VS. Force: The Hidden Determinants of Human Behavior* (Carlsbad, CA: Hay House, Inc., 2002), p. 246

Listening Softly

Many geniuses and inventors have acknowledged that their discoveries were *gifts* from *something* beyond their own thinking abilities. They acknowledge something greater than themselves. We all tap into something greater than our ego selves when we connect with our hearts and souls.

Remember those times you had an *insight* that seemed to come from *nowhere*—especially when you couldn't seem to find an answer after spending hours, days, or weeks trying to figure it out in your mind? Have you ever had goose bumps when you heard something you just *felt* was true without having to think about it? This is what happens when you listen from your heart, and it is very different from listening through the filters of your thought system. *Understanding* is a spiritual experience, not an intellectual experience.

Understanding is the key to natural joy and serenity.
Insight from within is the key to *understanding*.
Listening from your heart is the key to *insight.*

This is the cycle. It doesn't matter where you start; each facet leads in the same direction for positive results in your life and relationships—to serenity.

I suggest listening softly for a feeling from your heart because words are inadequate to express love, beauty, principle, or any other intangible truth. These truths can be understood only through your personal experience of them, which is beyond words.

Someone once asked Louis Armstrong to explain jazz. He replied, "If you can't feel it, I don't know how I can explain it."

Chapter One

The only purpose of words in this book is to point you toward the kind of *understanding* you will feel in your heart. If you can't feel it, you will not *understand it*.

Learning to ride a bicycle or walk a balance beam are good examples of *understanding* through feeling it. No matter how many times you heard an explanation of the concept of balance, it was beyond your comprehension until you *felt* it for yourself. Now you can hop on a bicycle and feel balance without even thinking about it.

Remember when you were trying to learn math principles? At first it didn't matter how many times you added 2 + 2; it didn't really make sense. Then, suddenly, you caught on and could add any combination of numbers because you finally *understood* the principle. It then made sense that 5 + 7 was the same as 4 + 8.

The principles of math and balance do not provide answers. They simply show you how to find answers or how to discover mistakes and make corrections. Similarly, the principles explained in this book do not provide answers. They show you how to *understand* and correct errors in your thinking that may be keeping you from connecting with your heart where you will find your truth—your answers.

Have you ever said, "I love you with all my heart and soul?" Why didn't you say, "I love you with all my mind?" At some intuitive level you know that there is something deeper and more profound in your heart than in your mind. The four principles explained in this book will help you recognize your thought system for what it is (without judgment), and to dismiss it through *understanding* so you can live from your hear and soul and experience your natural good feelings.

Another reason for listening softly is that words can actually keep you from accessing your heart when they get stuck in your thought system. Each person hears words from his or her own frame of reference and interpretation. For example, your mental picture of a dog is different from that of your friend's mental picture. This is why discussions of religion and politics are often avoided. These topics trigger so many differing beliefs and emotions about what is *right* and *wrong* that we stop listening except to the chatter of our own beliefs that are deeply embedded in our individual thought systems.

Words can sound so hollow and intellectual, whereas the experience of what the words are trying to convey can be so full. Listening softly—from your heart wisdom instead of your thought system—helps you get past the limitations of words to experience insight from your inner wisdom. You will know you are listening from your heart when you read something and have that "aha" feeling of insight that leads you to a higher *understanding* that makes even more sense to you than the words.

Listening from your heart can make the traditional definition of words seem topsy-turvy. For example, I once believed that forgiveness meant I should do something noble from my intellect. Through *understanding* forgiveness becomes a non-issue. When I drop my judgments and move into my heart, there is nothing to forgive. Forgiveness feels more like an awareness of the truth about my illusions, my inappropriate judgments, or a feeling of compassion rather than something to do. I experience the true meaning of, "Thou shall not judge," and of, "Forgive them, they know not what they do."

Some people hear principles intellectually, with just enough understanding to give them *lip service*. When they truly *understand*, they give *heart service*. Lip service often includes *shoulds* and *shouldn'ts*. "I should feel more gratitude." "I shouldn't judge others." Heart service just naturally bobs to the top inspiring you to do what you do based on passion and joy. Judgment (of yourself or others) isn't even a consideration.

The four principles, soon to be explained, help you remember how to bypass the limits of your programmed thought system so you can experience truth from your heart. I say "remember" because you were born with that ability and used it as a child before it was covered up by your developing thought system.

Remember when you didn't hold grudges and how quickly you could forget your disappointments and joyfully experience life again. *Understanding* the four principles will help you experience that childlike joy and fresh approach to living again. However, it may take time to get past the power of your thought system. Be gentle with yourself and keep listening softly.

Will you be able to live from your heart and soul all the time once you *understand* the four principles? Not unless you are a saint. Eventually, however, you will stop judging yourself when you find yourself living from your thought system and will simply dismiss your thoughts and experience your joy—over and over.

Reading this book could be like putting together a puzzle. Sometimes one piece makes no sense until it fits with another. Perhaps something you read in the middle or at the end will give you insight to make the beginning more understandable. Many people, including me, find greater *understanding* every time we read it. It is so easy to slip into the pattern of seeing the world through our programmed thought systems (after all, they have been with us for years) that we need some kind of inspiration to lead us back to the connection with our hearts and souls.

Several people have told me that they keep a copy of this book on their bedside table and reread parts at random. They claim that they always seem to choose just the right section they need to help them through whatever they are struggling with at the time.

Like math and balance, before *understanding*, principles can seem complicated. After *understanding*, they seem beautifully simple. When you listen softly, you will notice the chatter of your thought system, but you won't pay as much attention to it. Instead, you will listen from your heart. When you hear the principles in your heart, you will *understand*; and you will experience love, joy, and serenity in your life.

Keep listening softly.

2

A Treasure Map

Wayne Dyer tells a wonderful story in his tape serious *Secrets of the Universe*[1] that captures the essence of the human predicament and why we may need a treasure map to lead us back to our inner joy and serenity.

Once there were two alley cats. The young cat spent his days frantically chasing his tail. One day the old alley cat wandered by and stopped to watch the young cat running around and around in circles. When the young cat stopped to

---

[1] Wayne Dyer, *Secrets of the Universe*, Nightingale Conant Corp., The Human Resources Company, Chicago, IL

catch his breath, the old cat asked, "Would you mind telling me what you are doing?"

The young cat explained between panting breaths, "I went to cat philosophy school and learned that happiness is in the end of our tails. I know that if I chase long enough and hard enough, I am going to catch a big bite of happiness."

The old alley cat reflected, "I have not been to cat philosophy school, but I know it is true that happiness is in the end of our tails. I have observed, however, that if I simply wander around enjoying my life, it follows me everywhere I go."

How many of us run around in circles tying to catch a big bite of happiness somewhere outside ourselves. We could learn much from the wise old alley cat. Too many of us get caught up in the search for happiness and forget to be happy. I say *forget* because you already know how to be happy, but your innate knowledge may be buried and unused. Buried knowledge is like a well-kept secret that may require a treasure map to help you find it again.

Inherent good feelings are like corks in water naturally bobbing to the surface unless weighted down or buried under debris. Although good feelings are natural in human beings, too often they are buried under the debris of a thought system taken too seriously (something most of us have become adept at). An *understanding* of the four principles removes the weights and the debris so that wisdom, gratitude, joy, and serenity can bob to the top.

Some people don't believe they have inherent good feelings of joy, wisdom, and peace—or may believe it but feel frustrated when they think they can't access these good feelings. They may feel blocked and imprisoned within their own minds—as indeed they are when they don't *understand* how a programmed thought system works and how to get beyond it. The four principles

Chapter Two

(coming soon in chapters four through seven) serve as a treasure map that shows the way to open the prison doors and journey to the kingdom of heaven within.

I know you have heard it said that happiness lies within. Yet how often have you really experienced what that means? My guess is that your heart recognizes the truth of these words, so why do you keep forgetting what you know at your deepest level and keep looking for happiness outside yourself? Why do you question your innate worth—a preposterous thought that creates so much grief and misery for so many. The answer again: because you don't *understand* the power of your thought system and you listen to your ego (a product of your thought system) instead of your heart. Only your ego can lead you to believe that you can find happiness outside yourself.

Have you ever experienced inspiration after hearing or reading beautiful words of wisdom and vowed to be better, only to feel disappointed in yourself when you did not maintain those inspired feelings? Have you sometimes remembered what you *should* do, but didn't feel like it because you were too caught up in your anger, your hurt feelings, your judgments?

When this happens, you are following the dictates of your ego instead of your heart. When you see what you are doing and fall into discouragement and self-blame; you are still listening to your ego. There is nothing wrong with anything you are doing or have done. They have all given you experiences to help you know what works and what doesn't work. It is all good. And, your journey to joy and serenity will be much more pleasant when the first thing you give up is self-judgment and learn to love yourself-warts and all as discussed in Chapter 9.

Your ego may be objecting right now—fighting for its existence. Avoid the fight. Love your ego and then listen to your heart and read on. The treasure map in this book will help you stay on course to serenity, or help you get back on course when you inadvertently take a detour. Most of us, including me, take detours quite often. These detours don't feel good. The feelings compass chart (Chapter 5) will help you understand what is taking you in the wrong direction (away from your joy). This awareness may inspire you to dismiss the thoughts that create your discomfort and experience the wisdom from your heart that will take you in the direction of your joy again—instantly.

When you listen to your heart you will feel compassion when you *catch yourself* in the ego trap. You may even feel delighted at the opportunity for yet another life lesson that enhances your personal and spiritual growth. I have found it helpful to say fondly, "Oh there you are you cute little devil." My ego loses its power and I then have access to my heart again.

You'll find that happiness lies right under
your eyes back in your own back yard.

Chapter Two

This cartoon is almost correct. Since the kingdom of heaven is within, happiness is even closer than your back yard.

When you are disconnected from your heart, you (along with millions) may be caught up in the rat race of trying to find happiness outside yourself. You may be running in circles, like the young alley cat, trying to prove your worth. You may think you'll feel worthwhile if you make enough money, earn enough degrees, find the perfect relationship. Soon, you become so busy that you are not aware of the life you were meant to live—a life of love, joy, and serenity.

When you reconnect with your heart, you know you have nothing to prove. When your inherent good feelings are uncovered, you will live naturally in a happy, loving state of being. You will be connected to your inner guidance and will understand your passions in life and will follow them with joy and excitement.

Does *understanding* mean you will live the rest of your life in total bliss? Well, some people have reached that state, but I'm not one of them. Some people reconnect to their hearts, find serenity, and never waver. Most of us, however, are continuously seduced by our egos and thought systems.

Someone once asked, "So what is the point of all this?"

My answer: "To be happy."

Someone else said to me, "Well, sure you're happy. Look at all you have."

"That is my point," I replied. "I had everything I have now before I learned about these principles, and still I wasn't happy. I paid more attention to my illusions of insecurity and a false need to prove myself than to my inherent good feelings."

This explains why so many people who have achieved fame, fortune, or other forms of success as defined by our society, are often dissatisfied. They are misled by their thought systems to believe they can find happiness outside themselves and become deeply disappointed when they achieve material wealth, success, a dream relationship—and still aren't happy.

Does this mean you should live in poverty? No. Many people live from their inner passion and joy, create material wealth, have wonderful relationships, and are very happy. There are no *shoulds* about having or not having material possessions. However, there are principles that will let you know the source of your creations and which source leads to joy and which source doesn't.

The source of your stress, fear, anxiety, boredom, anger, depression, or any of the other feelings that keep you from joy and serenity, is your thought system. The source of your joy is your heart and soul.

At this point you may be wondering why I don't just get to the four principles. Listen to you heart. You may be ready to skip to those chapters right now. Or, you may be so disconnected from your heart that you need more groundwork in preparation for the four principles. You may just be curious and like to read every word. It is all good.

For deeper *understanding*, you may find it helpful you to start a journal. The first question to contemplate: How are you choosing to live your life? Do you live your life with serenity and peace of mind; or do you live in stress, anxiety, dissatisfaction, disappointment, anger, or depression? Are you one of the thousands who use antidepressants, illegal drugs, or alcohol even though these substances bring only momentary relief? Perhaps you are one of the many who expects to find happiness through material objects, power, or other people, only to become addicted to the need for more—more power, more relationships, and more things. You may be searching, searching, searching, but never finding.

Perhaps you have been well trained in effective coping skills. This can be very helpful since coping is certainly better than not coping. However, it brings only temporary relief until the next problem arises. Coping is like bailing water when you don't know how to plug the hole in the boat. (Of course, bailing is much better than sinking.) The exciting news is that the four principles show you how to plug the hole, how to reseal the boat. You don't need to learn how to *cope* with stress or anxiety. You can eliminate these states of mind whenever you choose.

In his book, *The Book of Secrets: Unlocking the Hidden Dimensions of Your Life,*[2] Deepak Chopra says it very simply:

> *Keep before you the vision of freeing your mind, and expect that when you succeed at doing this, you will be greeted by a stream of joy.*

Because we have well established thought systems it is normal to get hooked into old programming and become lost in our illusions. This is why the treasure map provided by the four principles is such a liberating gift. We can always find our way back home—to our inherent good feelings and inner guidance.

Most people need to be reminded over and over that *understanding* the principles does not mean that they will never get off course into some form of unhappiness. It does mean that they will soon realize they are off course and can use the treasure map to point them back in the direction of their inherent good feelings whenever they are ready. Like any often used map, the direction

---

[2] Chopra, Deepak, *The Book of Secrets: Unlocking the Hidden Dimensions of Your Life,* Random House, New York, NY 2004

soon becomes so natural that it is easier to find the way even without a map.

However, just as detours can take you away from a familiar road, you may often find yourself in a detour away from your inner wisdom. A programmed thought system is much more complex than a highway system. Ruts and sinkholes (old buried decisions and beliefs) may hook you and lead you astray.

Perhaps you are not truly being led astray; it could be part of a perfect plan to experience separation from serenity so that you can learn more life lessons. When you *get lost* the treasure map will help you find your way back home with a bonus feature—to help you find treasures in your *lost* time. One of the reasons for revising this book is that I have learned to appreciate the value of the lessons and gifts that can be found in *detours*.

I'm sure you have noticed that some people get very angry when they have to take a highway detour. Others see detours as an adventure and an opportunity to discover something new. People who don't find the gifts and lessons in their life experiences often stay angry, get depressed, or act like victims. Life becomes a matter of coping instead of an ongoing opportunity for joy and discovery.

Even though positive feelings are inherent within everyone, life presents many lessons for us to learn. Once you understand this, you can be open to the lessons instead of being paralyzed by fear, anxiety, or anger when you encounter opportunities to learn. In later chapters, you will learn how to see problems as friends with wonderful life messages. As you learn to recognize this possibility, the fear, anxiety, and anger vanish while the messages remain.

An *understanding* of the four principles has been such a gift in my life and in the lives of friends, clients, and others who have come to *understand* them. Even when we get lost in our thought systems there is a sense of knowing that we have simply taken a detour by taking our thoughts seriously for awhile. We don't stay on the detour for long when we realize what we are doing. The more we enjoy our natural good feelings, the less tolerant we become of the stressful states of our thought systems.

If we do *seem* stuck for long periods of time, we know that we may need help to heal some deeply embedded (though inaccurate) beliefs based on some past thoughts and decisions that are beyond our awareness. However, all healing processes are enhanced when based on an *understanding* of the four principles.

In the following poem, Sue Pettit captured what happens when we re-connect with our hearts:

Coming Home[3]

Coming home to peace and quiet.
Coming home to feelings warm.
Coming home where there's a fullness,
    where love in me is born.
Coming home's a simple journey,
    takes no movement on my part.
Instead of listening to my thoughts,
I listen with my heart.

If you are ready for joy and serenity, the four principles of psychological functioning[4] will serve as a treasure map that will

---

[3] Sue Pettit, *Coming Home*, available from The WV Initiative for Innate Health, Robert C Byrd Health Sciences Center, 1 Medical Center Drive, PO Box 9147, Morgantown, WV 26506-9147

[4] Originally formulated by Rick Suarez, Ph.D, and Roger C. Mills, Ph.D, *Sanity, Insanity and Common Sense: The Groundbreaking New*

A Treasure Map

lead you to your heart and soul whenever you are ready. This treasure map is one of the most valuable gifts I have ever received. It has helped me uncover the buried treasure within myself and to get back to it when I *forget*. It is my hope that this treasure map will help you find lasting peace of mind, joy, and serenity within yourself.

Happy treasure hunting!

Approach to Happiness (New York: Ballantine, Fawcett Columbine, 1987.) Out of print.

3

Are you Afraid of Serenity?

Many have become so disconnected from their natural state of being (joy and serenity) that they are actually afraid of it. Some may think serenity could be boring? Others don't want serenity because they would rather hang on to their dramas, their anger, their self-righteousness, their depression, their victim mentality. They don't *understand* that subconsciously they *think* they gain some benefits from choosing to live from the beliefs of their thought system rather than the wisdom of their hearts.

Others believe that the only way they can have serenity is to give up everything they have accomplished or learned or want? They fear that serenity means giving up control? If you ask,

Are you Afraid of Serenity?

"Would you rather have peace or your anger?" some will choose their anger. They really believe that revenge is better than forgiveness.

If you have any of these concerns or beliefs, you do not *understand* serenity. Serenity is not what you think—literally, as you will see in chapter four.

Serenity comes from the Latin serenus, which means clear, cloudless, untroubled. It does not mean stagnation, nor does it mean total passivity. In fact, serenity is the birthplace for creativity, wisdom, and meaningful productivity. And what, you may ask, is meaningful productivity?

That depends on what you are listening to—your ego (channeled through your thought system) or your true self (your heart and soul). Ego led productivity leads ultimately to emptiness. "Is that all there is?" Heart led productivity leads to joy and contentment.

Instead of lacking productivity when you return to your true state of being, you will know exactly what to do to fulfill your deepest desires and passions. You will not be scurrying around trying to fill some vague void. You will have nothing to prove. You will no longer be a slave to your ego, or to the ego of others. You will listen to others with interest, but not as a measure of who you are. You will stop worshipping the god of "what do you think of me?" Instead, you will have the wisdom to know, "What is right for me?"

I believe it is the natural desire of the human spirit to live in a state of gratitude, joy, compassion, and serenity. When you reconnect to your heart, you will not be bored. You will not be spending your whole day meditating in the lotus position (although you will find some meditation very helpful and soothing). You will not be

Chapter Three

in constant quiet seclusion. Instead you will experience deep *understanding* of your true self and how to achieve anything you want through the *Law of Attraction*. (See Chapter 5.)

Living in a state of serenity does not mean you will never experience sadness, disappointment, and other emotions. You will—and your heart and soul will comfort you and help you *understand* higher purposes and life lessons in everything that happens.

Sometimes you will forget everything you *know* and will slip back into the influence of your ego. I still do. I will keep reminding you of this because most people find it so discouraging instead of normal considering the long-standing habits we have developed through living from our thought systems. However, once you *understand* what is happening, you will lose your tolerance for the ego state of mind and won't want to linger there for long.

It is important to note that your soul does not demand attention as does the ego of your thought system. However, your soul will always be there for you when you choose to connect. In his book, *A Hidden Wholeness: The Journey Toward an Undivided Life*, Palmer J. Parker[1] provides a lovely metaphor that describes the nature of the soul.

What sort of space gives us the best chance to hear soul truth and follow it? A space defined by principles and practices that honor the soul's nature and needs. What is that nature, and what are those needs? My answer draws on the only metaphor I know

---

[1] Parker, J. Palmer, *A Hidden Wholeness: The Journey Toward and Undivided Life*, Jossey-Bass, A Wiley Imprint, San Francisco, CA 2004, pages 58-59

Are you Afraid of Serenity?

that reflects the soul's essence while honoring its mystery: the soul is like a wild animal.

Like a wild animal, the soul is tough, resilient, resourceful, savvy, and self-sufficient: it knows how to survive in hard places. Yet despite its toughness, the soul is also shy. Just like a wild animal, it seeks safety in the dense underbrush, especially when other people are around. If we want to see a wild animal, we know that the last thing we should do is go crashing through the woods yelling for it to come out. But, if we sit patiently at the base of a tree, breathe with the earth, and fade into our surroundings, the wild creature we seek might put in an appearance.

I believe the soul is anxious to show itself whenever we are ready, but it will not demand attention. It is the illusions of our thought systems (in the form of fear, anxiety, judgment) that demand attention until we *understand* and let them go.

Not too long ago I experienced a substantial financial loss. My stomach was in knots for several hours. In the past, this would have led to prolonged fear, self-flagellation for my mistakes, and depression. Instead, it wasn't long before I remembered my *understanding* of the principles in this book and I felt gratitude instead of depression. I quit focusing on my loss and focused on my many blessings and soon experienced my natural, joyful state of being.

I admit that I was once afraid of serenity. My ego fought for survival. However, I have lost my tolerance for feeling *bad* and quickly use my feelings compass to lead me in the direction of thoughts that feel good. I will forever be grateful for the principles that taught me to *understand* who I really am. I look forward to sharing these principles with you.

4

The Principle of Thinking as a Function

We are finally here. You have read a gazillion references to your thought system and it is now time to talk about how it is formed and how to use it as your servant instead of your master. The first question we need to ask is, "What is a thought?"

A thought is something you think. It is not reality, but it creates *your* reality. Thoughts are illusions yet they have the power to create misery or joy. A thought is pure energy and attracts like energy (as discussed further in Chapter 5.). Thoughts have the power to destroy the world or to create peace in the world.

The next question is, "How can something with so much power, be so misunderstood?"

It seems to be a well-kept secret that thinking is a function not a reality. *Understanding* that thinking is a function (or ability) is the key to *understanding* everything else in life.

You may be thinking, "That's not a secret. Everyone knows that thinking is a function." Actually, very few people really *understand* this principle. Instead, they believe that what they think is reality. Most act as though they are passive receivers or victims of their thoughts rather than the creator of their thoughts.

I love the bumper sticker that cautions: *Don't believe everything you think.* Most people do; and when they do, they become servants to their thought systems instead of masters of their thinking ability.

In the movie *2001*, scientists create a very sophisticated computer for their space mission. This computer has so many human qualities that it is named Hal. Hal is an amazing servant until *it* develops the human quality of an ego. Then Hal stops being a servant and takes over the spaceship.

Hal provides an excellent metaphor for what we do as human beings. We are born with a remarkable brain that can be an amazing servant. However, through conditioning from out childhoods, our cultures, and our personal perceptions and decisions we created a programmed thought system. The trouble begins when we forget we created it and allow it to become our master. The plot thickens when we don't even know we have become servants to the thoughts we created. We become allies or victims of the misery that is often caused when we believe in our thoughts as reality. We believe in them only when we don't *understand* that thinking is a function, not a reality, and allow our programmed thoughts to block our natural good feelings.

Our tests show that you are allergic to your negative thoughts.

This cartoon is funny because it is true. We are all allergic to our negative thoughts. When you truly *understand* this, you will stop taking your negative thoughts seriously. You will know they are just thoughts.

You may be wondering, "But what will happen if I don't think, or if I don't take anything I think seriously." Thinking is not the problem. The source of your thinking can be the problem. When you stop taking thoughts and beliefs that you formed in the past seriously, you will use your thinking ability to experience all the positive thoughts that naturally form from your inner wisdom (and *Universal Consciousness*).

The Brain as a Computer

The brain is like a computer (not really, but you'll get the point) that requires software to be useful and a person who understands how to operate it. Using your programmed thought system is the same as using old, outdated software full of bugs. And it can be as frustrating as trying to operate a computer without understanding the basic principles or reading the instructions. Both produce unsatisfactory results, to say the least. You are now reading an instruction manual to gain an understanding of the principles that can help you eliminate or bypass old, outdated software in your thought system

Many people do not realize that their thoughts and beliefs from the past are not *them*, just as software is not the computer. I have seen several versions of a cartoon showing a person smashing a computer because it wouldn't *work* properly. When we take our illusionary thoughts and beliefs seriously, we are using as much sense as the cartoon character. We forget that it is not our hearts and souls that are full of bugs. It is our thought systems that are full of bugs, and we smash ourselves instead of fixing our software. The wonderful part of this analogy is that simple awareness (*understanding*) is all it takes to fix our software—to eliminate the bugs that keep us from experiencing our inherent joy.

If you are like many who first hear this principle, your mind may be going crazy right now because you are trying to figure it out from your thought system instead of your heart. As Einstein said:

"We can't solve problems by using the same kind of thinking we used when we created them."

Computer buffs know what happens when they try to feed new information into a software program not designed to understand it: the computer beeps and flashes error messages, or even worse, "fatal error." A software program simply cannot accept what it is not designed to accept.

Your brain often does the same thing with new information that could be very useful to you. When you try to filter this information through your thought system, it beeps and says, "Wrong!" Fortunately, you have something a computer does not have—a heart full of inner wisdom to let you know what new information is useful to improve your life and relationships and what information is not useful. However, you don't have access to your inner wisdom until you dismiss your thought system—which happens automatically when you truly *understand* the principle of thinking as a function. Dismissing your thought system does not leave a void; it clears your channel to your inner wisdom so your thinking ability can be used to express your natural good feelings and messages from your heart.

What do you mean, you don't accept negative programming?

Chapter Four

Unlike the computer that won't accept negative programming, our brains will. Another major difference between humans and computers is that computers cannot function without software. Humans function best without their thought systems.

Personal Software (Your Programmed Thought System)

Computer software is written by people with knowledge of computer language. The computer industry is mushrooming as knowledge increases and applications multiply. Old software is thrown out as improved software is designed. Wouldn't it be wonderful if we would throw out our old software when it becomes outdated? Actually, that is what happens when we dismiss our thought systems and live from our hearts. However, there is a reason we sometimes don't dismiss our thought systems, or that it doesn't always last when we do.

The largest portion of our programmed thought systems were created when we were very young and lacking in knowledge. We started at an early age to create a thought system made up of our own perceptions and interpretations as well as thoughts we accepted from others. We were very trusting when we were young; usually believing what anyone told us. Unfortunately, much of what we were told consisted of beliefs passed along from generation to generation.

Many of the beliefs passed on were full of *shoulds* and *shouldn'ts* that contained judgments of worth or worthlessness. We were told how we *should* be in order to be liked and to be successful. We were also told how others *should* be and how life *should* be. We, others, and life hardly ever fit these beliefs, so we live with a sense of failure, pseudo-success, anxiety, stress, or disappointment in ourselves, life, and others. This was not done maliciously; our families and friends would not pass on trouble-some beliefs if they knew what they were doing. Not knowing any better, they themselves accepted beliefs passed on to them when they were young.

In her book, *A Return to Love*, Marianne Williamson confirms what happens when we forget that we create our own thought systems and egos through faulty beliefs of our own or others:

> *Thought separated from love is a profound miscreation. Its own power turned against ourselves . . . The ego has a pseudo-life of its own and, like all life forms, fights hard for its survival. The ego is like a virus in the computer that attacks the core system.*[1]

Not all beliefs that are passed on are harmful. Many come from the heart and are inherent in the beliefs of every culture: love, gratitude, forgiveness. These beliefs could be lived purely if they weren't contaminated by faulty beliefs and judgments from the thought system. It is the thought system that changes *the spirit of the law* to *the letter of the law*.

This doesn't mean that the thought system is *bad*. Our thought systems contain helpful information and skills such as reading, writing, arithmetic, names, phone numbers, and other useful information than can make life easier and more enjoyable. This information is factual and does not create negative emotions; we use it for our benefit rather than against ourselves.

Another reason the thought system is not *bad* is that you couldn't remember the faces of those you love without it. Your

---

[1] Marianne Williamson, *A Return to Love* (New York: Harper Paper-backs, 1992), p. 35

thought system also retains information about what feels good and what doesn't feel good. The trick is to use your thinking ability to dismiss troublesome thoughts and enjoy the thoughts that feel good.

All experiences are filtered through the function of thinking. We encounter problems when we create a thought system filled with old perceptions and decisions that act as filters to keep us from living life in the moment. We think these old beliefs are reality and stop listening to the messages from our hearts. Our natural good feelings can't get through. The principle of thinking as a function helps us *understand* when our thought systems are serving us and when they are harming us. When we *understand*, we can bypass our thought systems and let the good feelings flow. Albert Einstein said it this way:

> *The intuitive mind is a sacred gift; the rational mind a faithful servant. We have created a society that honors the servant and has forgotten the gift.*

What You Think is What You Get

We are free from the tyranny of the thought system when we *understand* that what we think determines what we see — even though we often make the mistake of believing, in an upside-down way, that what we see determines what we think. There is a popular saying, "I'll believe it when I see it." But the truth is reflected in the title of a book by Wayne Dyer, *You'll See it When you Believe It.*[2]

If it seems that I am going on and on about this principle, it is because I know this can be the most difficult one to

---

[2] Wayne Dyer, *You'll See It When You Believe It* (New York: William Morrow, 1989)

understand. Most people try to figure it out from their programmed thought systems. The filters of the thought system created the distortions in the first place, so it is impossible to see things differently through the same perspective. Thus, I am saying the same thing over and over in different ways in hopes that you will *listen softly* and that one of the explanations will sneak past the filters of your thought system and reach your inner wisdom where all great discoveries and new learning takes place.

Since we have so much to gain, why is it so difficult to connect with our hearts (before it becomes easy)? David Hawkins says it this way:

> *The attainment of wisdom is slow and painful, and few are willing to relinquish familiar views (even if they're in accurate); resistance to change or growth is considerable. It would seem that most people would rather die than alter those belief systems that confine them to lower levels of consciousness . . .* [3]

Do you know people who would rather die than give their up beliefs—who would rather remain in the dungeon of their perception prison than live in joy? Could that be said of you?

Looking at life through your programmed thought system can be the same as looking at the world through extremely dark glasses labeled "judgment," "blame," "expectations," "pride," "ego," "anger," "shoulds," and other forms of insecurity based on distorted thinking. These glasses are like blinders and filters that

---

[3] David R. Hawkins, M.D., Ph.D. *Power VS. Force: The Hidden Determinants of Human Behavior* (Hay House, Inc., Carlsbad, CA 2002) p. 235

destroy your view of life. The distortion can become your reality and shut out everything else, including the truth.

Are you wondering, "What is the truth?" The truth is what you see when you take off the dark glasses (dismiss your thoughts) and access the wisdom of your heart.

Have you noticed how different everything looks when you replace judgment with compassion, complaints with gratitude, and hate with love? Whenever you have any negative feelings, you can recognize that you are wearing one of your pairs of dark glasses. As soon as you take them off (dismiss your thoughts), your reality will change.

Sometimes you may be aware that you are looking at the world through those dark glasses, but you can't seem to drop them because they feel stuck on with superglue. It may seem as if you are stuck in your thought system. Knowing what is happening, even when you can't seem to get out of it, shortens the stuckness tremendously. It is only thinking about your stuckness and taking it seriously, obsessing about it, or beating up on yourself, that allows it to hang on and get worse. It helps simply to realize what is happening and wait for it to pass rather than to worry about it. It might help to go for a walk, read a good book, meditate, or take a nap. This can be difficult to do if you take your thoughts with you. It is calming when you know you are simply waiting for the thoughts to pass.

Not a Matter of Right or Wrong

It bears repeating that *understanding* the principle of thinking as a function does not imply there is a right or wrong way to think. *Understanding* the principle simply teaches you the many possibilities that come from thinking.

Your thought system is not *bad* anymore than California is bad when you would prefer to live in Florida. Actually, that is not the best analogy because your ego and thought system are part of you. To say they are bad would be to say you should judge yourself and fight with yourself. The point of *Understanding Serenity* is to eliminate judgment and war (even internal wars) or whatever it is that causes you stress and misery.

Instead of thinking in terms of right and wrong, or good and bad, think in terms of *preference* and *understanding*. Do you prefer stress (feeling bad), or do you prefer serenity (feeling good)? That question is not as silly as it may seem. This is where *understanding* comes in. When you *understand* that the source of your thinking (your heart or your thought system) determines your state of mind and being, you can choose your preference. It is a matter of *understanding* the source of your thinking and where it is taking you. Sometimes it is very simple. *If you don't like what you are thinking about, stop thinking about it.* Use your thinking ability to process the thoughts that come from your heart and you will feel good.

Chapter Four

Again I'll admit it isn't always easy. I used to obsess over certain thoughts—even when I *knew* better. When I finally got miserable enough or lost enough sleep, I would remember to quit listening to my thought system and would listen to my heart. Then, I would *see* things very differently and would regain my joy and serenity. You'll notice that I'm using past tense. My *understanding* has now deepened to the point that I don't entertain negative thoughts for much longer than a few seconds. Be patient with yourself and enjoy the journey. All your experiences lead to greater understanding—eventually.

Four States of Thought

When first learning about the principle of thinking as a function, many people find themselves in variations of the following states of thought.

Four States of Thought

1. Being caught up in thoughts and taking them seriously.

2. Being caught up in thoughts, but not taking them quite as seriously because of an *understanding* that they are just thoughts.

3. Being at rest. Dismissing thoughts and getting quiet to wait for inspiration from inner wisdom.

4. Inspiration—when you are experiencing life from your heart and soul.

You may find yourself in several variations of these states of thought throughout the day. *Understanding* the principle of thinking as an ability simply lets you know what is happening.

Chapter Four

Awareness Invites Change

When you *understand* your programmed thought system for the filter that it is, you will be able to bypass it, except for occasional short visits. When you *understand* what happens when you are there, you won't want to linger in your thought system for long. Each visit will simply confirm that thought system thinking does not produce happiness and peace of mind. Staying stuck in states 1 or 2 may let you know that you have some healing to do. Healing subconscious thoughts will be discussed in later chapters.

Remember that thinking is a beautiful gift through which you experience the beauty of life. You are almost always thinking. *Understanding* helps you dismiss thoughts that create problems in your life so that you can experience those thoughts coming from your heart which allow you to live in love, joy, and serenity.

Chapter Four

5

The Principle of Feelings as a Compass

Your feelings serve as your personal compass, letting you know where you are on the treasure map to joy and serenity. Unconditional, positive feelings (joy, contentment, love, compassion, wonder), let you know that you are experiencing life from your heart and soul. Negative feelings let you know you are off course into your programmed thought system.

The Origin of Feelings

Unconditional good feelings and actions flow naturally from your heart and soul. The feelings come first and are then experienced through the function of thinking. Negative feelings are experienced when you unwittingly tap into old beliefs stored in your thought system. *In other words, if the feeling comes first, it is from the heart; if the feeling comes second, it may be from your thought system.*

For example, you see a newborn baby and your heart is filled with wonder. The feeling of wonder comes first and then is processed through your function of thinking. On the other hand, you may have fearful thoughts about negative conditions in the world. You see a newborn baby and feel sad because of what this poor child will have to live through. Your thoughts create your feelings. It is typical for negative feelings to be based on fears from the past or fears of the future. Natural good feelings are a product of *being* in the here and now. (I wish we had more words to describe feelings. A feeling that is triggered from your subconscious may seem to come first, but it is based on thoughts from your past that formed a belief that was stored in your subconscious.)

Soon after learning this, I had an experience that illustrates how thoughts create feelings. During a one-week seminar where I was learning about the principles, I called home to see how my children were doing. I was informed that my thirteen-year-old son had been suspended from school.

This is how he told the story: "I found some cigarettes in my locker. I don't know how they got there. I was just putting them in my pocket to take them to the principal when a teacher came by and took me to the principal."

Chapter Five

My thoughts went crazy for a few minutes (actually, I created crazy thoughts): "He is lying to us. I'm a failure as a mother. If he's smoking cigarettes, he's probably also using alcohol and drugs. He is going to ruin his life. What will people think? I was very upset, so my feelings compass let me know, loud and clear, that I was caught up in my thought system and was not seeing things clearly. I dismissed my feelings compass instead of my thoughts and used more thoughts to bury my inner wisdom: "Yes, but this is different. These are really terrible circumstances over which I have no control. How could I possibly see them differently? I am going to have to scold him severely, ground him for at least a month, take away all his privileges, and let him know he is ruining his life." Fortunately, I had too much faith in the principles to take those thoughts seriously for long and inspiration quickly surfaced. I then saw the circumstances in a completely different way and felt understanding and compassion for my son's view of the situation. He had just entered junior high school where the pressure is enormous to follow the crowd rather than to follow common sense.

When I arrived home, I listened to my heart and knew what to do. I sat down with my son, put my arm around him, and said, "I'll bet its tough trying to figure out how to say no to your friends so you won't be called a nerd or a party pooper." He had been expecting my usual craziness and hardly knew how to respond to my sanity.

Tentatively, he said, "Yeah."

I went on, "And I'll bet the only reason you would ever lie to us is because you love us so much you don't want to disappoint us."

Tears filled his eyes, and he gave me a hug. With tears in my own eyes, I reassured him, "If you think you could ever disappoint us enough to diminish our love, then we aren't doing a good enough job of letting you know how much we love you, unconditionally."

I know it drives some people berserk to think this is all I did. I know because I have been there. "Did you just let him get away with that? You know he was lying; didn't you punish him? How are you going to control his behavior by being so wimpy?"

We can only guess what the results would have been had I followed my crazy thoughts to interact with my son. My guess is that my craziness would have inspired increased rebelliousness instead of closeness. In my heart, I know it is an illusion to think I can control the behavior of my son. The best I can hope for is to influence him in a positive way. My inner wisdom lets me know that he has a right to live his own life and learn his own lessons. I know he will have a much better chance to experience his inner wisdom if he feels unconditional love from me instead of my ego's need to judge and control him.

I am continually grateful for the principle of using my feelings as a compass to let me know when I am *off track.* Whenever I feel upset, angry, judgmental, disappointed, or any other negative emotion, I know that my feelings are being created by thoughts I am taking seriously. As soon as I recognize that and dismiss the thoughts, I am filled with my inherent good feelings and inner wisdom flows.

Dismissing negative thoughts is not the same as sticking your head in the sand. It is more like taking off blinders and filters so that you can see the situation from your heart. Sometimes the problem disappears along with the negative thoughts. Other times the problem may still be there, but you are able to view it differently and see solutions from your inner wisdom.

Feelings Compass Chart

The Feelings Compass Chart on the following page has helped many people use their feelings compass to increase their *understanding*.

The Feelings Compass Chart provides a graphic representation of the feelings and conditions you experience from your heart and soul and those you experience when thinking from your programmed thought system. In a nutshell, you feel good when thoughts are coming from you heart and you may feel bad when thoughts are coming from your thought system.

Try adding other words to the columns on the chart. A word such as *responsibility* feels like duty or compulsion when added to the thought-system column. Responsibility feels natural and easy when added to the heart and soul column. Notice how different *sex* feels in either column, or *charity, strength, giving, discipline, teaching, control, desire*, or any other concept you can think of.

Notice what happens when you take some of the words from the heart and soul column and add them to the thought system-column. *Love* and *forgiveness*, for example, do not have the same feeling when shifted. Have you experienced the contamination of love when you added expectations and judgments? Have you felt self-righteous for forgiving?

Again, I want to clarify that I'm not saying any of this is wrong. *Understanding* the principles gives you a road map to where you are; it doesn't tell you where you *should* be. I have already mentioned that there are gifts to be found and lessons to be learned from the experiences that come through your thought system as discussed further in Chapter 9.

FEELINGS COMPASS CHART

Heart and Soul	Thought System
High Level of Consciousness	Low Level of Consciousness
Security	Insecurity
Love	Hate or indifference
Serenity and happiness	Stress and coping
Productivity from joy and passion	Stressful productivity in search of happiness or to prove self-worth
Compassion	Judgment
Contentment	Wanting more, better, different
Wisdom	Rules, (*shoulds* and *shouldn'ts*)
Forgiveness	Blame, anger, self-righteousness
Gratitude	Blindness to miracles
Inspiration	Beliefs
Peace of mind	Depression and/or anxiety
The beauty of now	Past or future oriented
Natural positive feelings	Positive thinking
Law of Attraction	Law of Attraction

Chapter Five

Positive Thinking

Did you wonder why positive thinking is in the thought system column? Actually, positive thinking could be in either column, but I want to make a point. Positive thinking that requires effort comes from your programmed thought system. It involves trying to change thoughts instead of dismissing them and allowing natural positive feelings to surface automatically.

Positive thinking that requires effort is better than negative thinking unless it is conditional: "I will be happy only if I have positive thoughts," or, "I'm a success when I think positively and a failure when I don't." This kind of *positive thinking* creates stress and dissatisfaction. It is true that you will be happy if you have positive thoughts, but when positive thoughts come from your heart, they are natural and effortless.

The Law of Attraction

You'll notice that the *Law of Attraction* is the only phrase that is exactly the same in both columns. This is because the law of attraction applies whether it is coming from your heart and soul or your thought system. You attract into your life the exact energy you send out into the *Universe*—whether negative or positive. This has been said in many ways through the ages, for example: *you reap what you sow.*

As discussed in Chapter 4, thoughts are energy. The energy of your thoughts vibrates through your feelings. Those vibrations go out into the *Universe* and attract like vibrations. You get back what you send out. When you send out negative thoughts and feelings; that is what you get back. When you send out positive thoughts and feelings; that is what you get back. The law of attraction gives deeper meaning to the importance of dismissing thoughts that create negativity and allowing positive feelings to surface and attract more positive energy from the *Universe.*

If you have not seen the movie, *The Secret,*[1] I highly recommend it. This movie is changing the lives of many people (including mine). It adds to everything I know about the four principles discussed in this book.

This movie changed my thinking (and thus my feelings) about setting goals. In the past, I have resisted setting goals because it felt like adding "shoulds" and pressure to my life. I have been fortunate to *attract* so many opportunities into my life. I *thought* more goals would be overwhelming.

After watching *The Secret* and applying the law of attraction to the four principles, I experienced goals in a completely different way. There is a principle inherent in the law of attraction that helps you stay out of your thought system—the fact that you don't have to figure out how to accomplish goals that come from your inner passion. The *Universe* will provide. You will attract ideas and/or people who will help you accomplish these goals.

Understanding that goals did not need to include pressure, I did a meditation and had fun thinking of magnificent goals such as making money, and having books on the best seller list, and living in a house on the beach. I then just let go of all these goals and gave up all attachment—having faith that those that kept coming back to me would be in alignment with my inner joy rather than my thought system. All of them kept coming back to me with a sense of fun and delight instead of stress and pressure. I have been receiving ideas and opportunities that show me it is very possible

---

[1] www.thesecret.tv

to achieve these goals. I would have *thought* they were impossible if I had let my thought system stay in charge. Acting on these ideas is fun and exciting instead of burdensome and overwhelming. It is interesting to note that it doesn't really matter whether or not I achieve these goals. That is the paradox of the Law of Attraction. The happier you are in you are in the present, the more likely you are to attract more happiness and to do the things that will attract anything you want.

Understanding the Law of Attraction helped me gain a deeper *understanding* of using my feelings as my compass. I'm following the good feelings from my inner wisdom and am content whether or not these goals are achieved. My nineteenth grandchild was born during the completion of this book, and my inner wisdom is leading me to different goals—to spend as much time with him as I can during his first year.

Are All Negative Feelings Bad?

Just as thinking isn't bad, all negative feelings are not bad? Again, that would involve a judgment from your thought system. Your feelings compass simply gives you an awareness of where you are. (Understanding the law of attraction as discussed above may inspire you to give up your negative feelings sooner—so you don't attract more of the same.) Awareness is very different from judgment. You might experience something like this: I'm feeling very angry right now. I can keep feeling angry and feel miserable. Or, I can listen to my heart and see things differently—and feel good.

From my heart I can see a situation with compassion—for myself and others. It is amazing that when I listen to my heart, I see the other's point of view as well as my own hang ups based on some fear or false illusion. I don't have to *stuff* my feelings. They truly change when I experience the world from my heart. Wisdom follows and I know what to do to be loving and encouraging to myself and others.

A word of caution: Many people claim they are just following their feelings compass when they do negative things, such as *getting out* their anger or telling another person that their judgments about them are *the truth*. That is where your thought system will take you, not your heart and inner wisdom. Just as thinking comes from the thought system or from the heart; feelings also come from the thought system or from the heart. An *understanding* of this principle does not mean that you will never feel sad, hurt, or angry; it means that you can use your feelings as a compass to let you know where your feelings are coming from. When you access your heart, you'll know what to do.

Are All Positive Feelings Good?

Again, thinking in terms of good or bad requires a judgment. Simple awareness is more useful. It is possible to have good feelings from the thought system, but they may be conditional and temporary. You may feel great if you win the lottery, until you discover that money doesn't buy happiness. In fact, you may start to feel the anxiety of greed, the fear of losing it, the temporary joy (and ultimate misery) of focusing only on material things. You may feel good when you find your *true love* until you discover that many of those feelings were based on expectations and illusions from your thought system. True love is unconditional and everlasting.

Sometimes you may experience feelings from your heart or inner wisdom that *seem* similar to those from the thought system. While similar, they are totally different. As an example, I will paraphrase something I heard Wayne Dyer say in one of his lectures: "It angers and saddens me to see hunger in the world, but I know everything is in Divine Order. It is perfect that there is hunger in the world, and it is perfect that I want to do something about it." Instead of ranting and raving about the injustice of hunger, Wayne contributes regularly to the World Hunger Fund and does everything he can to raise the world consciousness to a level where hunger cannot take place.

Other so-called negative feelings may come from the heart, but the outcome will be different. You may feel very sad when you lose a loved one. However, along with the sadness will be gratitude for the time spent with that loved one. You will allow the sadness to teach you—perhaps to slow down and enjoy other loved ones in your life or to honor your departed loved one by living life to the fullest.

Too many people experience loss only from their thought systems, which then become hellish prisons. Parents who have lost a child go into depression and totally neglect their living children. Spouses who have been abandoned live the rest of their lives in anger, bitterness, or seeking revenge. They could not do this if they understood the power of their thought systems and dismissed them so they would have access to the wisdom of their hearts.

In a sense, all feelings are good and all thoughts are good when you consider that everything you think and do provides opportunities for learning and spiritual growth. Using your feeling compass can shorten the misery of thought system thinking by helping you recognize where your thinking is coming from.

Visualization and Affirmations

Visualization and affirmations can be very helpful to overcome the negative programming of your thought system. Visualization can help you re-program your thought system to be your servant instead of your master.

How is this different from positive thinking? It will be different when you seek the wisdom of your heart to determine your deepest desires and life purposes and then use visualization of these desires and purposes to overcome negative programming.

It is also different when you *understand* that thinking is a function and not a reality. You use the function of thinking to remember phone numbers and math principles. Why not use it to program the power of your thoughts to help you accomplish heart determined goals and desires.

Listening to you heart is the key. I have known many people who listened to motivation tapes and felt like failures because they couldn't accomplish what the motivators did. I have a theory about this. The motivators followed their hearts and their passions and achieved amazing results. Many people who listen to the tapes don't have the same passions—they just want the money, the success, the fame. They experience stress and disappointment because they are following their heads not their hearts. Others listen to motivation tapes to assist them in finding their own passions and experience joy and enthusiasm instead of stress and disappointment.

When you are experiencing any stress or unhappiness in your life, it may help to take a look at the Feelings Compass Chart. Allow your inner wisdom to let you know what thoughts or beliefs from the column on the right are causing you to feel bad. As soon as you "see" it, that *understanding* may allow you to drop those thoughts and access feelings from your heart. Love, joy, compassion, and wisdom will flow.

6

The Principle of Separate Realities

Another well-kept secret is the fact that everyone lives in a separate reality. This simply means that we all interpret things differently and that each of us views the world from his or her private logic. Again, this is not really a secret. We all know we see things differently, but tend to forget it and act as though everyone should think and feel the same as we do—I mean as I do.

A popular example that demonstrates the fact of separate realities is that everyone who sees an accident describes it differently. The reason becomes obvious when we *understand* that everyone sees the world through the filters of his or her own unique, programmed thought system. We have separate realities because everyone has personal memories, interpretations, and beliefs that act like filters through which present events are seen. When we view the world through these filters, it is impossible to see what *is* with a fresh perspective.

Most of us have heard about this principle, but we forget to apply what we know about separate realities in our relationships and create all kinds of problems about who is right; or we wonder why others are so dense they can't see things the way we do.

Hearing about separate realities and *understanding* this principle at a deep level are not the same. When you really *understand* the fact of separate realities, you will stop spending so much time and energy trying to change the reality of others. Instead you will be curious about their reality. You may find it interesting or surprising. You may not agree, but you will be respectful and/or compassionate. Another possibility is that you may not want to spend your time being around some people because the energy of their reality isn't a fit for you. However, you can make this choice in an honoring manner—both for your reality and the reality of others.

Phil and Lisa experienced separate realities soon after they were married. Phil was an *early bird*; he loved getting up at dawn full of energy and ready to enjoy the day. Every morning he bounded out of bed and sang loudly in the shower, hoping Lisa would wake up. Noticing her still in bed with the covers pulled over her head, he would noisily bounce on the bed as he put on his shoes and socks, thinking, "If she really loved me, she would get up and enjoy this time with me."

Lisa, totally annoyed at what she saw as his *inconsiderateness,* would be thinking, "If he really loved me, he would know I hate getting up early and would be quiet and let me sleep."

They often discussed their differences, but neither really *heard* the other because they were more interested in changing each other than in understanding each other. Both felt as though they were talking to a wall as they tried to make their points. What they did not realize is that they were talking to two walls—the wall of their own reality and the wall of the other's reality.

Christmases were a disaster. When Lisa was growing up, everyone in her family had received one very nice, expensive present for Christmas. In Phil's family everyone had enjoyed the fun of opening several inexpensive presents. So Lisa would buy Phil one nice, expensive present, and Phil would buy Lisa several inexpensive presents. Every Christmas they felt disappointed and misunderstood—both thinking that the other was too dense to know how to really enjoy Christmas.

We may be amused at Phil and Lisa for not seeing how simply they could solve their problems by respecting their separate realities instead of trying to change each other. Nonetheless, when dealing with our own precious beliefs, we are often just as blind.

Have you noticed how important it seems to tell others, especially those you love, when you think they are wrong? Then you wonder why they don't appreciate it.

Bill used to dread visiting his father because they both always ended up with bad feelings. Bill said, "We used to spend all our time together arguing about who was right and who was wrong. I was certainly never going to admit I was wrong because it seemed very clear to me that I wasn't. Dad would not admit he was wrong, even though I made every effort to let him know how old fashioned his ideas were. *Understanding* separate realities was a godsend for me. Dad and I no longer argue over our differences. I respect how he sees things and I know I would see them the same way if I were in his shoes. Now we just share the love and gratitude we have and enjoy each other's company."

Remember, there is a difference between understanding from an intellectual level (from your thought system) and *understanding* from your heart. When you forget about separate realities, you may tend to take everything personally. You may feel misunderstood if someone doesn't agree with you. You may feel hurt, self-righteous, judgmental—and many other feelings from your thought system. Doesn't it make more sense to feel compassion or interest? After all, what they say represents their reality, not yours.

I remember becoming obsessed with hurt feelings and self-righteous annoyance with a colleague who had different ideas about how to run a project. I made myself very miserable for awhile. One day while sharing my woes with a friend, she reminded me, "It is just what she thinks. You don't have to agree with her and you don't have to make her wrong." Duh!

I just love being reminded of these principles when I get lost in my thought system. As soon as I *understood* what I was doing, I tapped into some childhood memories where I lost my sense of self when my two older sisters told me (constantly) how stupid I was. I developed a belief that I had to fight for my sense of self. (This is a good example of an illusionary belief.) Through the gentle reminder from my friend, I quit feeling like I was six-years-old and was able to heal my old belief and forgive my sisters. I could see that all their "put downs" of me had nothing to do with me. It was just what they thought in their childhood minds and what they needed to do as they tried to figure out who they are in this world. I quit obsessing with hurt feelings and annoyance and was able to tell my colleague, "Hmmmm. I see it differently." We worked out a compromise that felt good to everyone on the project. (See more about healing your wounded child in Chapter 9.)

When you don't understand separate realities, you might wonder, "How could he possibly be like that or do that? They would be happier if they did it my way, liked my kind of music (especially at the volume I prefer), ate the foods I like, and loaded the dishwasher the way I do." These thoughts and judgments can create a great deal of misery in the form of anger, resentment, or other stressful emotions.

Without *understanding*, we become convinced that if we try hard enough, we can persuade others that our reality is the right one. This never works—so marriages may break up in hostility, parents and children experience power struggles or *generation gaps*, and nations go to war. The reverse can also apply. Some people think their reality is wrong or is not as good as others, and so they may spend a lot of time feeling inadequate, insecure, and depressed.

I had another opportunity to experience the difference between taking my reality seriously and dismissing my thoughts so I could hear wisdom from my heart. Again, I became very upset with one of my children. The details aren't as important as the lesson. I knew I was deeply stuck in my thought system and I couldn't seem to drop it. I kept wondering, "How could he do that? He is making a huge mistake." I couldn't understand how he could justify his behavior.

Finally, I sat down to meditate and ask for messages from my heart, which came almost immediately. The first was, *"You wonder how he could have done such a thing. How many times in your life have you done things that would invite the same question from others? How many huge mistakes have you made? It is his life to live and his mistakes to make."*

The message seemed so obvious once I *heard* it, but I couldn't hear it while stuck in the perception prison of my thought system. This story also provides an example of the mirror insight process (described in Chapter 9). Often, whatever we find annoying in someone else is really a reflection of an area where we need some work ourselves. We often don't want to see this, especially when we think that what the other person does is so much worse than what we do. With *understanding*, we can see the humor in this. If what we do is less serious, how much better our time could be spent correcting our own foibles than judging others.

Other messages from my inner wisdom followed: *Look at the trouble you create for yourself when you think others should live up to your expectations or do "what is right" and "for their own good" according to you.*

I had to laugh at my self-righteousness when I *saw* it. I had believed that my son's actions had made me miserable; instead I remembered that it was my thoughts about what he did that made me miserable. I felt gratitude for the lesson and compassion for my son—and for my parents who often made themselves miserable over my actions and mistakes. *When we truly understand the principle of separate realities, we see differences with compassionate interest.*

Visitors to another country usually respect separate realities; they certainly wouldn't be welcome if they told people of other countries that they should speak another language and change their customs. Traveling is enjoyable when visitors learn about different cultures and traditions and respect differences. Wouldn't it be wonderful if we approached personal relationships with the same wonder and respect?

You may be one of those who judge your own reality at times. One day when I was judging myself for not having a deeper understanding of the principles, I suddenly realized that any form of judgment would only block my understanding. When I stopped judging my present reality, I could see that to say I should be farther along than I am makes as much sense as saying a rosebud should be a rose in full bloom.

We are all in the process of evolving, learning, and growing (or refusing to grow). Getting in the way with our judgments only creates negativity and impedes progress. Can you imagine how much more helpful we would be to ourselves and others if we were loving and compassionate instead of judgmental?

A master gardener does not fret because her roses are not growing into petunias; rather she simply nurtures all of the flowers with water, weeding, and fertilizer so they can reach their full potential as roses, petunias, or whatever they are. We would have better relationships if we simply enjoyed and nurtured ourselves and others.

"Shoulds" are not necessary when we experience our inherent good feelings. From the heart, nurturing ourselves and others comes naturally. *Our inner wisdom lets us know that the key is to love and nurture, not to judge.*

Some people have incorporated this principle into their thought systems and misused it. I heard someone say in a disparaging tone of voice, "Well, that is just your separate reality, and I have a right to mine." This was not said from love, compassion, and respect. The principles (when truly understood) can never be used against others—or ourselves.

Crazy Thoughts–Yours, Not Mine

Illusionary thinking is often easier to see in others than it is to see in ourselves. I remember thinking schizophrenics were really crazy when they thought they saw little green bugs crawling up the wall, or when they believed they were Napoleon. It was obvious to me that those were crazy thoughts, whereas all my thoughts, naturally, were serious and real—even the ones that made me miserable.

Kimberly Kiddoo, a psychologist in Coral Gable, FL, who taught me so much about the four principles, had a client in therapy who believed a garbage truck was going to eat her. Kimberly spontaneously laughed and said, "That is a silly thought." She had spoken from her common sense and wisdom but felt a little embarrassed because she had been taught that it is inappropriate to laugh at something a client is taking seriously. (This happened before Kimberly knew about the four principles.)

Fortunately, the client heard the truth of her words at deeper level than they had been spoken and she began to improve significantly. Several months later Kimberly asked what had made the difference in her recovery. The client replied. "It was the day you told me my thoughts couldn't hurt me." (It wasn't really what Kimberly said but her client's *understanding* that was inspired by the words.)

One of my clients quit having panic attacks after hearing the story of the garbage truck. She said, "The last time a panic attack started, I knew it was just my thoughts. I laughed and felt fine."

We all have silly thoughts that we take seriously. Yet, <u>when we know they are just thoughts, they lose their power to hurt us.</u>

I know it isn't this simple for everyone. It wasn't for me. Some people *understand* sooner than others. As I have said before, it seems so difficult until *understanding* makes it so simple.

Some people insist that they must be judgmental to keep the world from "going to hell," and they put themselves in a state of mental hell—which does not help the world. If you cannot find it in your heart to love a negative person; at least love yourself enough to stay out of his or her way, without judgment. Our world expands greatly when we understand and appreciate separate realities. It is possible to enjoy differences (or at least understand them) instead of fighting over them.

If your programmed thought system is resisting, you are probably dredging up the worst possible examples you can imagine, such as murder, rape, and burglary—or a spouse who did something terrible. Understanding separate realities helped me understand what Christ meant when he said, "Forgive them. They know not what they do."

Self-righteousness, hatred, or any form of negative judgment only keeps you separated from your heart and inner wisdom that could lead you to positive action. When you live from you heart you will know what to do about these issues to get the best possible results. You will act from love and wisdom instead of perpetuating hatred.

You may argue, "But some things really are wrong!" Many wise people have taught, "What is, Is." This can be a difficult concept to understand, because it is void of judgment. What I know is that I can spend a lot of time making myself miserable about what I think are the injustices of the world, or I can make sure my world is as loving as possible. Byron Katie has written a wonderful book titled, *Loving What Is*[1] On page 1 she makes the following statement: *The only time we suffer is when we believe a thought that argues with what is. When the mind is perfectly clear, what is Is what we want.*

There have been several cases in the news where people have decided to forgive the person who killed a loved one. It is the only way they could find peace instead of misery. As Desmond Tutu said, "To forgive is not just to be altruistic. It is the best form of self-interest." It is natural to follow the *Serenity Prayer* when you wish to experience life from your heart:

> *God, grant me the serenity to accept the things I cannot change, the courage to change the things I can, and the wisdom to know the difference.*

---

[1] Byron Katie, Loving What Is, Harmony Books, NY, 2002

Chapter Six

It is so easy to get caught up in right/wrong thinking. As mentioned before, many people would rather be *right* than loved or loving. I had the opportunity to recognize that I was choosing to be *right* instead of loving when my husband and I were getting ready to come home from a large convention. He wanted to get in line for the hotel shuttle to the airport two hours early. I wanted to get in line one hour early. We were both getting annoyed at what we perceived to be obtuse behavior in the other. Each of us thought the reality of the other was ridiculous.

My feelings compass gave me a wake-up call, and I consciously chose to go into my heart. From that space I said to Barry, "I wonder what would happen if we looked at this differently and had compassion for what it would cost either of us to follow the lead of the other. The price I would have to pay to go early is the discomfort of spending more time at the airport. The price you would have to pay is worry and anxiety about being late."

When I saw it this way, it was obvious to me that it would be easier for me to change. From my heart, I saw his reality as endearing instead of wrong. I also saw the benefits of getting to the airport in plenty of time to relax. I saw how I could learn form him when I quit seeing his point of view as ridiculous.

It was contagious. Barry felt loved and responded by moving into his heart. He said, "Well, I guess I do exaggerate." We laughed, left for the airport early, and had a good time being together.

Being loved and loving is much nicer than being *right*. In the heart, where separate realities are seen with interest and compassion, loving has top priority.

The Principle of Separate Realities

7

The Principle of Mood Levels or Levels of Consciousness

We've all heard someone say, "I'm just not in the mood," or, "Let's wait until he's in a good mood." What do these phrases mean? Very simply, they mean that sometimes people feel good and sometimes they don't; and that it isn't much fun or productive to be around people who are in a "bad" mood.

Your thought system may create mood swings on a regular basis. You will never be in a low mood when you are coming from your natural inner happiness. And, of course, you experience a

The Principle of Mood Levels, or Levels of Consciousness

higher level of consciousness when you are connecting with your heart. Experiencing moods is another key to let you know where you are—in your thought system or in your heart.

Again, this is not a matter of judgment, but of awareness. Everyone experiences moods. Some people seem to fluctuate between extremes in moods more than others; but we all experience times when we feel good and when we don't. If you are willing to search for it, there is usually a *thought* behind every mood.

Some people say, "I'm just tired." Then they learn they have just won the lottery and suddenly they aren't tired any more. A couple may be arguing. Then the pastor comes to the door and their mood changes completely. There is nothing like a thought to shift a mood.

Have you ever noticed how different your own separate reality is, depending on whether you're feeling high or low? For example, recall the last time you were driving along in a good mood, and someone needed to cut in front of you, and you cheerfully waved him in while remembering how often you have been in the same situation. Then think of another time when you were in a low mood and stepped on the gas, determined not to let that person cut in front of you while you mumbled about how stupid and inconsiderate he was.

This principle can be an indicator or your level of consciousness. A low level of consciousness equals a low mood. A high level of consciousness equals a high mood level. It is illusionary thoughts (worry, anxiety, fear) from your thought system that create low moods.

When you are in a low mood, everything looks bad. You may feel overwhelmed and have feelings of impending doom. There seems to be no way out. Lower moods or levels of consciousness simply mean that you have lost perspective and *understanding* because you are living in your programmed thought system. A higher mood or level of consciousness simply means that you are seeing things with greater *understanding* from your heart.

I'm sure you have experienced both high and low moods or levels of consciousness and you are aware of how differently you function during each state of mind. Since high moods or levels of consciousness are obviously so much nicer, and you have experienced that state of mind many times, you may wonder why you don't stay there all the time.

Sometimes low mood levels just happen as part of our physiological functioning. When we don't get enough sleep or have enough to eat, we may experience a low mood. Research in biorhythms has shown that we experience intellectual, emotional, and physical cycles that peak and ebb.

When low mood levels are physiological, it makes sense to simply wait for them to pass, just as it makes sense to sleep when we get tired. Physiological moods are not nearly as bad as the thoughts we have about them. The analogy that describes this phenomenon is "making mountains out of molehills." Typically, however, it is a belief or thought that is the culprit in our mood swings—not physiology.

Often, we are unaware of the thoughts that have created our low moods. Trying to figure out the cause only makes things worse because we are trying to figure it out from the very thought system that created the low mood in the first place. Remember what Einstein said:

> *"We can't solve problems by using the same kind of thinking we used when we created them."*

The Principle of Mood Levels, or Levels of Consciousness

You will find peace when you use your low mood to let you know what is happening so you can shift to your heart. Your inner wisdom will give you insights and often make you laugh at the thoughts you were taking seriously.

I remember times when I was feeling inadequate and insecure about something and would retreat into a very low mood and call it depression. Then I would be upset with myself for being depressed, thereby feeling more inadequate and insecure. How depressing! I did not understand the vicious cycle I was creating with my thoughts. At times I looked forward to my depression because I used it as an excuse to lie in bed all day and read. Funny how my depression didn't last very long when I started enjoying it. I finally saw the obvious and realized that I did not have to get depressed in order to take a day to rest and enjoy myself.

A quiet mind is one of the best *cures* for a low mood. You automatically have a quiet mind when you dismiss thoughts from your programmed thought system. Another *cure* is to observe your thoughts fondly instead of taking them seriously. Sometimes the simple *understanding* that *it is only a mood* will be enough to raise your level of consciousness. The moment this happens your thoughts will be dismissed or taken less seriously and you will have access to your heart which will allow you to see things from a higher perspective. Your mood will change.

Ellen was upset because a department store had failed to refund her money as promised. She took out her anger on the customer service clerk, who talked back rudely to Ellen. As soon as Ellen realized what was happening, her mood shifted and she saw things differently. She then said to the clerk, "You really have a tough job, don't you?"

Chapter Seven

The clerk responded to this empathy immediately. "I sure do." From then on, she was very helpful and the problem was resolved. *Moods are contagious.*

It doesn't make sense to trust our thoughts or feelings when we are in a low level of consciousness. *Understanding* this principle teaches us to get quiet (verbally, physically, and mentally) and wait for the low mood to pass.

There have been times when I was upset with my husband and gave him the *silent treatment*. My thoughts were not quiet, and he could feel the angry energy emanating from me. This is not the kind of quiet I'm talking about. When I understood this principle, I would get quiet when I felt my anger, but it was a very different kind of quiet. I was in the process of dismissing my thoughts and waiting for messages from my heart. Barry enjoyed this kind of silent treatment. It was *a silent treatment for me* instead of *a silent treatment against him*. Don't underestimate the power of quiet to help you let go of illusionary thoughts so you can move into your heart.

Being caught up in your thought system is like being caught up in a storm. At the first signs of a storm, what do sailors do? They quickly take down their sails and wait for it to pass. What would happen if they left their sails up? They would have a big fight with the storm on their hands—a fight they would most likely lose. When you hang on to your thoughts, instead of getting quiet until they pass, you often have a big fight on your hands. If you have any negative feelings or fears, you are losing the battle. Try quiet.

Getting quiet is such an important concept that it is a sub-principle of mood levels and levels of consciousness. You will learn more about the importance of quiet in Chapter 11. Meanwhile, be gentle with yourself. It may take several days or weeks of quiet to help you reach your heart.

Meanwhile, looking for the life lesson or benefit of your situation may help. Again, this may be difficult in the beginning. Once you have an *understanding* of the four principles, and have experienced serenity, seeing life lessons comes more naturally. If you think another person has contributed to your low mood, using "the mirror insight process" might help—if you see your own *faults* with self-love, compassion, or humor. (More about *Mirror Insights* in Chapter 9)

Prolonged low moods may be letting you know that you have some *out-of-awareness* thoughts and beliefs that need healing. When you can't seem to access your own inner wisdom, it may be wise to seek the help of someone who has access to theirs—someone who understands the importance of leading you out of your programmed thought system and into your inner wisdom.

Now You See It, Now You Don't

Again, I want to emphasize that high or low moods (or levels of consciousness) are not a matter of judgment. Consciousness is a state of awareness, perspective, or insight. Sometimes you see it (*understand*), and sometimes you don't. The moment you *understand* that you are seeing things from a lower level of consciousness, you have jumped to a higher level of consciousness. It takes *understanding* from your inner wisdom to realize when you are not seeing something with *understanding*. However, if in the next moment you judge yourself because you didn't see clearly sooner, you flip right back into your head and lose your understanding. Be gentle with yourself. Stop judging yourself. (I know. I know. I'm still working on it. That cute and adorable ego of mine can be a real pest.)

You may ask, "But, what about all those times when I'm not in a good mood or at a higher level of consciousness. How do I get out of my low mood if I don't try to figure it out or use positive thinking?" This question indicates that your ego and your thought system are fighting for their *lives*. Again, be gentle with yourself. You have had a lifetime of practicing and perfecting how to live from your thought system. Old habits can be very tenacious. However, the fact that you have read this far indicates that your heart and soul are thrilled that you are *getting it*. You are hearing something or you wouldn't be struggling. Your heart and soul won't join the struggle. They will just patiently wait. They are always there for you—because they are the *real you*.

When you are in a low mood, take care of yourself the way you do when you get the flu. Low moods can change immediately with recognition, or, like the flu, they may hang around even when we know what they are. When we get the flu, we know that the best thing to do is to take care of ourselves until it passes. If we are considerate, we are careful not to spread it around. It is wise to treat low moods the same way. Think how much peace there would be in the world if people didn't spread their low moods around.

Sue Pettit had a wonderful insight about moods and the dangers of spreading them around. She was inspired to write a poem entitled, *Lily's Loose*. Notice the similarity of Lily Tomlin's role as Ernestine at the switchboard from the old TV show *Laugh-In* and what happens when we let our thought systems take over.

The Principle of Mood Levels, or Levels of Consciousness

Lily's Loose[1]

Lily is the operator at the switchboard of my brain.
And when she starts reacting, my life becomes insane.
She's supposed to be employed by me
and play a passive role.
But anytime I'm insecure, Lilly takes control.

Lilly's loose, Lilly's loose, Lily's loose today.
Tell everyone around me just to clear out of my way.
The things I say won't make much sense
    all COMMON SENSE is lost.
Cause when Lily's at the switchboard
    my wires all get crossed.
Lily is my own creation, thought I needed her with me
To organize and then recall all my life's history
But she started taking liberty with all my information.
And whenever she starts plugging in,
I get a bad sensation.

Lily's loose, Lily's loose, Lily's loose today.
Tell all my friends and relatives to clear out of my way.
I don't give hugs and kisses

---

[1] *Lillie's Loose,* From the book, *Coming Home,* by Sue Pettit, available from The WV Initiative for Innate Health, Robert C Byrd Health Sciences Center, 1 Medical Center Drive, PO Box 9147, Morgantown, WV 26506-9147

when I'm in this frame of mind.
And please don't take me seriously
it'd be a waste of time.

She looks out through my eyeballs
and sees what I do see.
Then hooks up wires to my past;
she thinks she's helping me!
When I'm in a good mood, I can smile at her endeavor.
But when I'm in a bad mood
Lily's boss, and is she clever.

Lily's loose, Lily's loose, Lily's loose today.
Tell the world to hurry by and stay out of my way.
I'm feeling very scattered—I'm lost in my emotion.
Lily's on a rampage, and she's causing a commotion.

I heard a wonderful story from a lady in Connecticut who said that she read this poem to her teenage son. Then, every time she would start lecturing or scolding, one of them would see what was happening and say, *Lily's Loose*, and both would start laughing.

Laughter

Laughter has the power to transform moods. Have you ever noticed that as soon as you can laugh at or about something, you see it differently? With *understanding*, it is difficult to take things too seriously.

In my parenting workshops, I suggest that parents quit taking things so seriously and adopt an "isn't that cute" attitude around some things that upset them. I'm able to give them a good example. I was driving myself crazy over the fact that my teenagers kept leaving empty cereal bowls in their rooms. Not only could I never find a clean cereal bowl when I needed one, but the bowls in their rooms were caked with dried cereal and sour milk. I took this very seriously and ranted and raved until my feelings compass let me know that I was in a very low level of consciousness. My thought system was running rampant. As soon as I dismissed my judgments, I really could see it as a cute, teenage phenomenon.

Then I was inspired to take action from love and humor. We discussed the problem at a family meeting. After laughing about how normal it is for teenagers to do things like this, we came up with a solution. Every other week, I would collect their cereal bowls daily as a reminder to myself and them of how much I love them. Every other week they would bring their cereal bowls to the dishwasher out of love for me.

Since I know how easy it is for teens to get distracted from things that are a priority to adults, we agreed that it would be fine for me to put a love note on their pillows when they forgot. This worked much better than all the ranting and raving—and was a lot more fun.

Nothing I did about the cereal bowls from my thought system was effective. Those actions created rebellion, anger, and frustration. None of us felt loved. What I did from my heart created love and harmony—and the solution was effective.

Gratitude

I have found that one of the quickest ways to change my mood is through gratitude. It is difficult to hang on to my silly thoughts while appreciating all there is to be grateful for.

Once I was in such a sour mood that I couldn't think of anything to be grateful for. Then I looked down at my hands and was struck by the absolute miracle of my ability to move my fingers. Then I looked up and saw the sky. How beautiful! *Love, beauty, and miracles are all around us whenever we are willing to notice.* When we are stuck in our thought system, we miss so much. We could be walking on a spectacular beach or through a beautiful forest and miss all the beauty if our focus was on the illusions of our thought systems. We miss the simple, though miraculous beauty of fingers, relationships, and the gift of life itself when we allow our thoughts to make us miserable.

Helping Others in a Low Mood

Techniques feel very different when coming from your heart than when coming from your thought system. The technique of reflective listening provides a good example. Reflective listening simply means to validate what a person is saying by reflecting the words (and hopefully the meaning) back to the speaker. If you do this from your thought system, it is likely that you will sound like a parrot. If you do reflective listening from your heart, you will experience compassion and will reflect feelings as well as the spoken words.

Also, you won't take the words of others so seriously when they are coming from a low mood or from beliefs from their programmed thought system. Their words are often a cover up for feelings of some kind of insecurity. You'll know that people you are listening to don't need *advice* from your thought system. They need compassion from your heart, as illustrated in the following example.

The Principle of Mood Levels, or Levels of Consciousness

Sally was very angry at her sister because of an argument that had taken place two years ago. The sister wanted to come for a visit, but Sally refused to see her. Her husband, Joel, gave her some *spiritual* advice. "Don't you think it is time to let go of your anger and learn to forgive? Don't you know how much this anger is hurting you?"

Sally did not find this advice helpful. She felt hurt and told Joel, "You just don't understand."

Joel shared what had happened with a friend who had an *understanding* of the four principles. She asked Joel, "What do you think would happen if you stopped seeing the details of what she is saying and instead saw her as a person who is caught up in her thought system and is in a low mood? Try giving her compassion through reflective listening instead of advice."

That night Joel apologized to Sally for giving her advice and said, "I can understand how hurt you felt by the argument with your sister."

Sally responded defensively, "It seems like every time I try to get close to her, she says something mean to me."

Joel said, "Sounds like you are feeling scared that she might hurt you again. Staying away is a good way to protect yourself from that."

Sally started to cry. She felt so validated. She hadn't known herself that that was what she was doing, but she realized it was true when Joel said it with such loving compassion. Feeling his love put her into her heart where she started to feel compassion for her sister and herself. "Donna is critical just like my mother was. We both do that. We hated it when our mother did it, but we now do the same thing."

Joel said, "Sounds like you understand that she may be scared too, and doesn't know how to break old patterns."

Sally said, "I hadn't really thought of it before, but maybe we could talk about it and help each other. We could remind each other when we notice we are doing old stuff and jokingly say, 'Knock it off.' I really don't want to repeat those old patterns. My mom didn't know any better, but maybe we can learn."

In this example, Joel helped Sally find her own solutions by avoiding advice. This often happens when someone experiences compassion from another. It is difficult to stay in a low mood when feeling loved, and from a higher mood we have access to our own inner wisdom.

Other people may not find their own solutions the way Sally did. That is not the point. The point is that people can't hear advice from others or from their inner wisdom when they are feeling discouraged. Compassion does not have ulterior motives. People need our compassion even if they stay in a low mood.

Conclusion

The principle of mood levels is an extension for your feelings compass to let you know when you are taking your thoughts seriously. In a low mood you don't feel so good. You can correct this by getting quiet and waiting for low moods to pass—or by knowing enough not to spread your bad moods around—or by forgiving yourself and others when you don't have enough *understanding* to wait for it to pass.

It now seems perfect to me that I get lost in my programmed thought system once in a while. I can find so many gifts in the experience. Of course, while I'm lost, it is impossible to see the gifts and it is not helpful to beat up on myself. *It is helpful to know that*

The Principle of Mood Levels, or Levels of Consciousness

it is normal and that I can't see it until I see it. Using the principles can help me and you understand what is happening and how to find our way back to our inherent good feelings. Why feel bad when feeling good is just a dismissed thought away?

8

What Thoughts Are You Giving Up Your Happiness For?

One day I put a nice oak table in the garage for storage. Other family members started putting their junk on the table. I nagged, "Please don't put anything on the oak table or it will get scratched." No one listened and eventually everything, from tools and bicycle parts to a worn-out car battery, was on the table.

Finally, I went into the garage and cleaned off all the junk so I could cover the table with something to protect it. Sure enough, it was scratched and gouged.

What Thoughts are you Giving up Your Happiness For?

I was angry! Fortunately, I had some errands to do so no one had to listen to me express my anger. I drove around totally lost in my negative thoughts—taking them very seriously.

Finally, my feelings compass let me know that my thoughts were making me feel angry and miserable. As soon as I became aware of what I was doing to myself with my thoughts, *understanding* took me to a higher level of consciousness and my mood changed. My natural good feelings surfaced and I had to laugh as I began to see things from the wisdom of my heart.

I realized that my family had not been irresponsible for putting things on the table; I had been irresponsible for not protecting it in the first place. Everyone who hears this story thinks it is funny that I didn't "see the obvious" and have enough sense to cover the table in the first place. This is the point. Silly thinking is usually obvious to anyone who isn't caught up in it. When we are caught behind the filters of our thought system, we really believe what we think and become slaves to our thoughts—no matter how much misery they create. However, happiness is just a dropped thought away.

To summarize again: when we are angry, all we see is a world full of bitterness. As soon as we use our feelings compass to let us know our thoughts are taking us in the wrong direction, we will *understand* that we are taking our thoughts seriously. When we let go of the thoughts that create the anger, our natural good feelings surface. We then see a world full of love, beauty, compassion, forgiveness, gratitude, and peace of mind. *What we think is what we get.*

As soon as I saw the oak table episode from my heart, more profound wisdom followed. I realized that I was living my life for scratches in an oak table when there were so many other possibilities. It was a beautiful day and I had been missing it. I had so many things to be grateful for and I was taking them all for granted. A question came from my heart: *What thoughts are you willing to give up your happiness for?*

Wow! How much of the beauty of life do we miss by staying in the illusions of our thought systems?

Circumstances

Many people still believe their happiness depends on their circumstances. We often hear people say things like "I'll be happy when I finish school, ... when I'm married, ...when I'm single, ...when I have more money, ...when I have children, or ...when you do what I want you to do." This is not true. Circumstances have nothing to do with happiness.

If you are not happy before you get what you want, you won't be happy after you get it—or at least not for long. People who think they are happy when they first get what they want find that happiness doesn't last long. When things settle down, they feel that old, nagging insecurity and dissatisfaction or get trapped back in their feelings of unhappiness the first time things don't go the way they *should*.

During a radio talk show discussion of these principles, one man called in and asked Dr. Rick Suarez, "Do you mean to tell me that losing my leg would not be a reason for me to be unhappy?"

He was told, "That is right. It is only what you think about losing your legs that could create unhappiness."

The caller replied, "That is the most stupid thing I've ever heard," and hung up.

A former patient of Dr. Suarez was listening and called in to report, "What the doc says is true. I lost both my legs in Vietnam, and I have never been happier. That doesn't mean that I don't wish I had my legs. I would love to have my legs back; but before I learned about these principles, I didn't know how to be happy when I had my legs. Now I know how to be happy even without them."

Circumstances look different when seen through the filter of your thought system. When you have peace of mind and contentment, you will see *what is* without judgment, like the wise man in the following story.

A Horse Story

Many years ago, a wise man lived in an old mountain village. One day a beautiful, wild stallion ran into his corral. When the villagers heard the news, they came to his farm and marveled, "What a wonderful thing! You are so fortunate!"

The wise man replied, "Maybe so, maybe not."

A few days later, the stallion broke the corral fence and ran away. When the villagers heard the news, they came to his farm and said, "What a terrible thing! What bad luck!"

The wise man replied, "Maybe so, maybe not."

The next day the stallion returned bringing a whole herd of mares. When the villagers heard the news, they came and exclaimed; "Now you are the richest man in the village, and surely the luckiest!"

The wise man replied, "Maybe so, maybe not."

The wise man's son tried to break one of the mares but was thrown and broke his leg. When the villagers heard the news, they came and sympathized, "What a tragedy! Who will help you now with the harvest? This is such a misfortune!"

The wise man replied, "Maybe so, maybe not."

96

The next day, the Cossacks came to get all the young men of the village to fight in their wars. They did not take the wise man's son because of his broken leg.

This story could go on and on. This old villager lived a concept taught to me by my dear friend, Max Skousen: *I do not know what is in my best interest.* This truth is very difficult for many to understand; but most of us have had something happen to us that we thought was terrible at the time and later realized was the best thing that could have happened. There is another way this has been said: "If you want to hear God laugh, tell him your plans." We never have the control we think we have, yet we find the gifts in every situation when we listen to our hearts.

Another humbling aspect of circumstances is to have the experience of feeling very sorry for yourself about something and then hearing about someone who has or is experiencing circumstances that seem so much worse. Suddenly, you realize that your circumstances are nothing in comparison and not worth worrying about. I don't mean to imply that there are *real* circumstances that make worry more valid than wisdom from the heart. The point is that even insignificant things can cause misery when seen through the filters of the thought system.

If attitudes were a product of circumstances, it would be impossible to find people who still celebrate life even with terminal cancer or other crippling afflictions. Many of us were deeply touched by Mattie T. J. Stepanek, who was afflicted with a rare form of muscular dystrophy that took the lives of his three siblings and kept him confined to a wheelchair and the almost constant need for an oxygen machine. He was an inspiration to many on the Oprah Show and through lectures that obviously came from his heart before he died in June, 2004, a few weeks before his 14th birthday. His poetry books, *Loving Through Heartsongs*, *Celebrate Through Heartsongs*, *Journey Through Heartsongs*, and *Hope Through Heartsongs*, inspired many. Mattie provided just one example of many who continue to live in serenity no matter what their circumstances.

Some people live as though life is a celebration—something to enjoy fully. Others live as though life is a chore—something to endure. There is a popular poster expressing this attitude: "Life is hard and then you die." Which is it—a celebration or a chore? The answer depends entirely upon what you think.

There is a story about two boys who caught a bird and created a plan to fool the village wise man. They decided that one of them would hold the small bird in his hand so the wise man could not see it. They would then ask the wise man if the bird was alive or dead. If the wise man said it was alive, the boy would crush it to death. If the wise man said it was dead, the boy would open his hand and let the bird fly away.

So, they stood in front of the wise man and one boy said, "My friend has a bird in his hand. Is it dead or alive." The wise man said, "That, young man, entirely depends on you."

Heaven or Hell: It Depends on You

We can think anything we choose to think. Our emotions and actions are a direct result of what we choose to think. We have the ability to create *heaven* or *hell* through our thinking ability. Thinking from our thought systems often creates hell. Thinking from our hearts and souls creates heaven.

The beliefs and interpretations some people accept or create can seem so real that they live and die for them even when they make no sense. These beliefs and emotions are the source of hatred, prejudices, war, unwillingness to forgive, the misery of revenge cycles, and all insecurities. As explained in the *Law of Attraction*, we create what is going on in the world through the energy of our thoughts and feelings. In Wayne Dyer's book, *Gifts from Eykis*, Eykis points out:

> *Thinking is the basis for every single major and minor difficulty you encounter. The problems that arise in politics, religion, education, families, business, the military, society, medicine, and every form of human enterprise are due to self-programmed, unreal thinking.*[1]

Any form of insecurity, stress, or anxiety results from creating thoughts that produce certain emotions and then believing those thoughts and emotions are reality rather then simply products of our thinking. Try feeling insecure without thinking that you are insecure. It is impossible. You must think you are insecure before you feel insecure.

To see this even more clearly, consider the following examples. Joe feels inadequate. He believes his inadequacy is real, and does not recognize it as just a thought. His inadequacy exists only because he believes it is real. He then bases his behavior on that thought and acts inadequate. This is why it is not helpful simply to tell Joe he is adequate. Your beliefs will not change Joe's beliefs about himself. Joe will feel adequate only when he quits taking his thoughts seriously and re-connects to his heart so his natural feelings of adequacy can bob to the surface.

---

[1] Wayne Dyer, *Gifts from Eykis* (New York, Pocket Books, 1983), pp. 118-119

What Thoughts are you Giving up Your Happiness For?

In the next example, Melissa believes she is depressed because life is overwhelming. But life itself is not overwhelming; only what she thinks about life makes it seem overwhelming.

This statement can bring up all kinds of debate: "What about disasters, death, war, and so on?" The point I am making is illustrated by two people who experienced an earthquake. One was living in fear and trying to figure out how to move out of earthquake country. The other said, "This helped me realize what is important in life. I don't need all the things I lost in the earthquake. This event was a wake-up call for me to enjoy the more important things in my life, such as family and the simple pleasures."

Some might say, "But what if she lost her family?" The point is illustrated again by two people who lost loved ones. One person went into depression and could not imagine living without her loved one. Another person (after a normal period of sadness and mourning) said, "What a gift it was to have had Bill in my life for the time we had together. I miss him terribly—and still, I feel blessed with the gift of life and all there is to enjoy. Don't be surprised if you hear me talking to Bill. His spirit is still with me."

As mentioned before, emotions from the heart are not always positive?" Certainly the experience of grief is a very real part of the human condition. However, these feelings are appropriate to the situation at hand and do not last forever unless they become embedded in the thought system. Natural good feelings and joy will surface when thought system thinking ceases.

Some have argued, "Good feelings are not natural to me. It is more natural for me to feel stressed or depressed. I don't try to feel these things, they are just naturally there." For these people it can be difficult to get past their personal beliefs and accept the fact that there is a thought (obvious or hidden) associated with every feeling. Others may think they *should* control their thoughts to find happiness.

Controlling your thoughts is not the point. The truth is that hanging onto any of the thoughts that keep you from your natural happiness is giving up control to your thought system.

Understanding is not the same as control. *Understanding* leads to effortlessly letting go of thoughts that create problems because you know they are just thoughts. And, as I keep reminding you, *understanding* can come and go due to the conditioning that created such a strong thought system during your childhood.

When first learning about these principles, I believed that *understanding* meant I would never have negative thoughts again; and I became very disappointed in myself whenever I took my thoughts seriously. By doing this, I had flipped out of my heart and into my head, where I used this information against myself.

However, my feelings compass would let me know this and that it was time to stop thinking about my "failure" and to get quiet. Before long, *understanding* would lead me back to my inner wisdom where I learned that it didn't matter if my negative thoughts kept creeping in. (They were not actually *creeping* in. We become so proficient at instantaneously pulling up *files* from our programmed thought system that we forget they are still our moment-to-moment creations. It then seems that thoughts creep into our mind beyond our control, which is impossible.) Eventually I experienced just *observing* those thoughts without judging them. I even felt a tolerant affection for my negative thoughts. I started seeing them as interesting or humorous or cute and adorable. When I understood that they were just thoughts, they could not hurt me.

What Thoughts are you Giving up Your Happiness For?

Most of the time, I could laugh and dismiss them. I now know that when it seems I can't dismiss them, they could be a blessing in disguise waiting for me to use them as opportunities for greater learning and healing by treating them as friends and learning from them. You will learn more about healing your conditioning in the next chapter.

Dismissing your thoughts through *understanding* may be second nature for you by now. However, if you need help at times, it may be effective to ask, *"What thoughts am I giving up my happiness for?"*

Sometimes this question is enough to take you to a higher level of consciousness. As soon as you *understand* what you are doing, you will automatically dismiss thoughts you are giving up your happiness for and will experience your inner happiness bobbing to the top like a cork in water.

If you are still hanging on to your thoughts, try having compassion for your conditioning and see if you can understand what you *think* you gain by hanging on to your thoughts.

Have compassion for your old conditioning

When you do not experience *understanding*, it may help to have compassion for your old conditioning while answering the following questions: Does it seem as though hanging on to your thoughts benefits you? Perhaps you believe that forgiving others would be condoning what they did and that not forgiving them is the only way to keep them from hurting you again. Could it be that you believe revenge is sweet—that you really will feel better if you hurt others back and make them pay for hurting you? Do you mistakenly believe you are okay only if you are look better than someone else? Are you one of those who would rather be *right* than *loving?* What else can you think of that seems like a good reason to hang on to thoughts that keep you from your happiness—thoughts that don't really feel good? Wouldn't you rather have thoughts that make you feel good?

That may seem like a silly question, but it is interesting that our thought systems create a distorted view of gratification. We may feel "gratified" for thinking we are "right." We may feel "gratified" for what we think we gain by being a victim. We may feel "safe" by doing all we can to avoid what we *think* would be rejection from another person. This kind of gratification has a doubled edged sword that leads to ultimate misery.

Awareness of your mistaken beliefs may help you have a change of heart (*understanding*) so you can dismiss the beliefs that don't feel good so you can experience your natural happiness again. If you are still having trouble dismissing thoughts that don't feel good, it may be helpful to accept them as friends with something to teach you.

Accepting your thoughts as friends with something to teach you

Be aware of the thought or feeling you have and embrace it. Then ask, "What do you have to teach me?" The first time a dear friend suggested I go for a walk with my "fear" about something, and treat my fear as a friend, I thought she was crazy. I couldn't imagine why I would want to treat my fear as a friend. I trusted my friend so I tried it and was surprised at how quickly my fear gave me some messages and then went away. I can't remember the messages now, but I was very impressed that my fear could teach me and then go away. Once you have learned from your thoughts, you may experience the exhilaration of loving them and letting

What Thoughts are you Giving up Your Happiness For?

them go—and feeling your natural happiness bob to the top. If not, *Seeing the Gift in Every Situation* or the *Mirror Insight Process* in the next chapter it may help.

You have power over your programmed thought system when you understand, observe it (instead of judging it), and then dismiss it—not when you try to control it. Dismissing your programmed thought system does not mean denial or repression. It means *understanding* that thinking is a function—not a reality. When happiness is more important to you than any thing else, you will be happy because there will be no thought you will be willing to give up your happiness for. You will do whatever it takes to get out of your thought system and into your heart. When you don't have understanding, love yourself exactly where you are, unconditionally. If loving yourself unconditionally is easier said than done, you will find help in the next chapter on *being aware of the miracle of you.*

9

Be in Awe of the Miracle of You

The greatest gift you can ever give yourself is to love your-self unconditionally—*to be in awe of the miracle of you.* If you find this easier said than done, what keeps you from loving yourself unconditionally? Do you find yourself getting hooked into the detour of caring too much about what other people think about you? Do you get hurt and angry when others don't live up to your expectations? Do you beat up on yourself when you make mistakes? Are you still running old tapes of things you heard as a child? Do you take spiritual truths, run them through your thought system, turn them into "shoulds"—and then get caught up in self-judgment when you don't live up to your own expectations of yourself? The list could go on and on. Do you know of anyone who is perfect and never does any of the above?

Did you know you are not supposed to be perfect? What would you have to learn if you were perfect? Why would you need this earth school if you were perfect? *Understanding* that you are not supposed to be perfect can help you relax and lovingly accept your imperfections as wonderful opportunities to learn—and to enjoy the learning process.

Since most people don't understand that they aren't supposed to be perfect, a lack of unconditional self-love seems to be part of the human condition. It has been a big part of my life experience, and I know it has been a big part of yours, since it is normal for everyone.

We all handle this lack of self-love differently. Some spend their lives trying to prove they are loveable through pleasing or accomplishments. Some hide from their feelings through drugs or television. Some depend on a relationship to make them happy — and then blame the other person when this doesn't work. Some spend hours in a therapist's office trying to figure out why they are so unhappy. Some live in a self-made hell of anger, resentment, and victim mentality. Others choose a spiritual path to find peace and serenity. *All of these paths can lead to personal growth when we are willing to learn from our experiences.* The latter is a part of your journey or you wouldn't be reading this book. However, even a spiritual journey will not bring lasting peace and joy until you learn to love yourself unconditionally.

You may have found love, peace, and joy through *understanding* the four principles. And, like me, you may find yourself taking lots of detours away from serenity. Recently I have learned that all of my detours center on my lack of unconditional self-love. And, I have learned some ways to get beyond these detours and enjoy loving myself-warts and all.

I would like to take you on some journeys that may help you love and accept yourself—no matter what. The first is a meditation to meet your soul. I know you can't close your eyes and read at the same time; so I'll tell you about the mediation and you can do it later if it appeals to you.

Meditation to meet your soul

Close your eyes, get comfortable, take several deep breaths until you reach deep relaxation. Then imagine you are sitting in front of your soul. Take time to bask in this presence and to experience all of the following questions.

What does your soul look like?

What does it feel like?

What are the characteristics of your soul?

Feel the love of your soul.

Feel the compassion of your soul.

Feel the joy of your soul.

Spend as much time as you like enjoying your soul.

When you are ready, ask your soul what it would like you to know right now.

What message does your soul have for you about the mistakes you make?

What message does your soul have for you about the thoughts you are hanging on to.

What messages does your soul have for you about life and love?

When you are finished, gently come back into the room. Get your journal and write about your experience. Share this experience with others. Don't keep your soul a secret. *Your soul is you.* How could you not love you?

When I did this meditation, the first thing that surprised me was that my soul was not inside my body as I have always thought. It was a huge, turquoise energy that surrounded me in love and compassion. It was clear to me that my soul and I are one, and that I have all the beautiful qualities and characteristics of my soul: love, compassion, joy, generosity, wisdom, passion, and serenity. How could I not love myself?

Then I saw that my thought system and I are also one and that it has a lot to teach me. Right now it seems that the biggest lesson to learn about my thought system is to love myself whenever I get hooked into the mischief it can create—and to keep learning. One way is use the *Mirror Insight Process.*

Mirror Insight Process

If you believe everything you have read so far, yet still can't let go of your negative thoughts about something or someone; welcome to the club—and to the possibility of seeing your negative thoughts as an opportunity to learn more about yourself. Your negative thoughts may have a message for you that can provide you with a very important life lessons in order for healing to take place. One way to see the message is to look in an imaginary mirror and see yourself as a reflection of the person or situation that has you hooked. How are you like the person you are angry at? How do you do some of the things you are judging in the other person? It doesn't help if you use what you see to judge yourself. It does help when you can see the humor in what you are doing, let it go, and experience the compassion that follows.

Chapter Nine

I learned a great lesson on a flight from Germany to Los Angeles. I did not want to check green roll-on luggage and a small duffle. I stored both pieces in the rack above my seat and settled down to read my novel.

Before take-off, I heard an announcement from a flight attendant that they had a green roll-on bag that would have to be put off the plane if it was not claimed. I remember thinking, "That could be mine: I wonder if I should check it out." I dismissed the possibility, however, because I knew my luggage was stored in the rack above my seat.

Then I heard my name over the loudspeaker announcing that I should come claim my luggage. The two people strapped into their seats next to me had to get up so I could struggle out to the aisle and seek a flight attendant. Another passenger hurried up to me and told me that the man behind me had taken my luggage out of the rack so that he would have room for his things. She was furious because he had left my luggage in the aisle and everyone had to climb over it. I couldn't believe it; but sure enough, when I went to the front of the plane, there was my green suitcase. I explained to the attendant what had happened, but there was not time or space to do anything except have my bag checked.

I was so angry at this man that I went back to my seat and confronted him: "What made you think you had the right to take my case out of the rack?"

He calmly explained, "It was above my seat, and you are supposed to put your luggage under your seat." (He hadn't bothered to notice that the rack over his seat also extended over my seat.) I was incensed, and still couldn't believe it, nor could my fellow passenger who had told me what had happened. She joined me in confronting him. We let him know that we thought he was inconsiderate, selfish, and arrogant. He shrugged it all off as though it were nothing.

I sat in my seat and fumed. I tried to tell myself, "Let it go. This is just your thoughts and they are driving you crazy. Your anger isn't hurting him, but it is certainly hurting you." I remembered one of my favorite, anonymous quotations: "*Anger does more damage to the vessel in which it is stored than to the object upon which it is poured.*" I also remembered all the scientific research about the damage that anger does to the body and to the immune system.

None of that helped. I continued to think about the audacity of this man. I could not understand how he could possibly justify his actions.

After dinner, I met several passengers in the aisle by the restrooms, and they all fed my self-righteousness. One man said, "What a jerk." I loved it. The woman who had already spoken to me said she was still so angry that she couldn't enjoy her meal. I loved it. I went back and told the man off some more.

Can you believe that someone who has written a book on *Understanding Serenity* could act this way? What about dismissing the thought system and accessing inner wisdom? What about using my feelings as a compass to let me know that I was taking my thoughts very seriously?

Well, eventually I did pay attention to my feelings compass, and now I'm thankful to the man who gave me such a wonderful opportunity to learn more about myself and to heal the beliefs that were causing my misery.

I decided to do a meditation and try the *Mirror Insight Process* to see what my anger was telling me about myself. My first glimpse in the mirror was to see that I had been a bit (just a bit) selfish and inconsiderate myself to bring two pieces of luggage onto the airplane. If everyone did the same, there wouldn't be enough storage room. It was easy to gloss over my own selfishness when his seemed so much worse.

Notice that last statement. This is the kind of thinking I can use to excuse myself from changing. "If someone else is worse, they are the ones who should change." The truth is that if my faults are not as bad, it could be easier for me to change. From the thought system, it makes more sense to point fingers instead of changing myself. From my heart and inner wisdom, I feel humility and drop my judgments.

This small insight, from looking into the mirror, took me into my heart where I felt gratitude to this man for giving me such an excellent opportunity to see myself. Whether or not he was right or wrong for moving my suitcase became a non-issue when I started to understand the message and life lesson my anger had taught me. I felt compassion for both of us. I had to laugh at the drama I created from my thought system. I also felt grateful for the *Mirror Insight Process*, which so often helps me find the gift in every situation.

Seeing the Lessons or Gifts

There are many master teachers and scientists who teach that there is *divine order* to everything. Perhaps shifting back and forth between your thought system and heart increases your appreciation for happiness and peace of mind. Perhaps you could not learn important life lessons any other way.

Another time I was using my thought system in a way that was making me miserable because I thought a friend was being inconsiderate. I was upset; my stomach was churning; and I couldn't sleep as I counted my grievances. Finally, I paid attention to my feelings compass and wisdom surfaced from my heart. I saw clearly that I was giving up my happiness for some negative thoughts. Then I had a *mirror insight* and learned a beautiful (and funny) lesson. *Which is worse, being inconsiderate or being judgmental?*

I had to laugh at my self-righteousness. Then I saw that it was not even a matter of being better or worse because being inconsiderate and judgmental are both simply aspects of thought-provoked insecurity.

Perspective and compassion quickly followed as I remembered the many times I have been inconsiderate either because I didn't know better or because I *believed* I was justified. I also realized that just because I thought this friend was being inconsiderate didn't mean she was; it meant only that she was not living up to some rules and beliefs *I had created* from my programmed thought system. (Have you noticed that if someone thinks you are being selfish, it is usually because you aren't doing what they *selfishly* want you to do.) I laughed at those thoughts also and could then feel love and gratitude for my friend—and for myself. I had learned, again, that it is silly to have thoughts that I'm willing to give up my happiness for.

More recently I was angry at my husband, Barry, because he didn't answer his cell phone. I felt like having a temper tantrum because I couldn't reach him when I wanted to. This time my anger didn't last long before I asked, "What am I making myself so miserable about? What lesson could I learn from this?" When I looked for the gift, I saw what I needed to learn about myself very quickly. I can be a slave to my phone—thinking I have to answer it whether or not it is convenient for me. When I dismissed my thoughts that created the anger, I wanted to follow Barry's example and use my cell phone as a convenience instead of becoming a slave to it. When gifts aren't so obvious, it could be that you are responding to an out of awareness belief from the past.

Healing Beliefs from the Past

In my parenting workshops, I point out that children are always making decisions (at a subconscious level) about who they are, what the world is like, and what they need to do (how they need to behave) in this world to thrive or to survive. Since many of these decisions are made on the basis of a child's fear of disapproval and/or punishment, many decisions have to do with surviving instead of thriving. These decisions form beliefs that may have made sense when we were children. The problem is that we hang on to these beliefs (old software) when they are outdated and no longer serve us. Valerie Seeman Moreton describes this process in her book *Heal the Cause:*

> *Anytime we make a decision with great emotion attached, it becomes the subconscious "rule of action" from that time forth. This means that when an upset occurs, even at a very young age, like one or two, a decision is made (subconsciously) that influences the rest of your life. If that decision was that you were "not loved" or "not good enough," your whole life would be about compensating for that belief to prove it was false. Behaving in a particular way to get love or approval can cause self-defeating patterns to develop and defense mechanisms to form. And all of this is based upon a lie, founded upon fear instead of love.*[1]

---

[1] Valerie Seeman Moreton, N.D., *Heal the Cause* (SanDiego: Kalos Publishing, 1996)

Many defense mechanisms (beliefs) take the form of misbehavior. Through experiential activities (where parents role-play their children), adults gain an understanding about how the thought system is formed—theirs and their children's. They also learn that the best way to help a *misbehaving child* change beliefs and behaviors is through love (encouragement), not fear (punishment). Love (kind and firm parenting) can take both parent and child out of their thought systems and into their hearts where they can focus on loving solutions instead of fearful blame and punishment.

You don't experience fear when you access your heart or spiritual source. Fear comes only from the illusions of old programming. When you have difficulty *dismissing* old, outdated programming, it could be that subconscious decisions and beliefs have not been brought into your awareness and healed.

Changing Your Blueprint for Living

You created a *blueprint for living* based on the intelligence, perceptions, decisions, beliefs, and maturity of a three-year-old. And, you may still be having three-year-old temper tantrums—adult style. This blueprint for living is based on your thought system and seems to be written it stone. Isn't it funny (or scary) to realize that you may be living your life based on the thinking and lifestyle planning of a three-year-old? Fortunately, your feelings compass can help you bypass your thought system and create new blueprints for living based on the wisdom of your heart.

Meanwhile, that *three-year-old* can be very tenacious. Thus, you may get off course into your thought systems on a daily basis. So keep your feelings compass handy. As soon as you see your temper tantrums as humorous, they lose their power and wisdom

114

surfaces. When you can't see your temper tantrums as humorous, you may need help.

Seeking Help

Sometimes your programmed thoughts and beliefs are so deeply embedded that they keep causing you problems—emotionally, physically, and spiritually. Dismissing your programmed thought system may give you temporary relief, but those subconscious beliefs keep returning and affecting your behavior and your health. You don't even know what thoughts you need to dismiss. They are beyond your conscious awareness. You are, however, profoundly aware of the misery they cause.

There is a wonderful story about a little girl who went to camp. During the day and evening, she was enthralled with all of the activities, new friends, and story telling around the bonfire. However, that evening a counselor found her crying in her bed. The counselor tried to comfort her in every way she could think of, without success. Finally, she said, "Do you know that God is always with you?" The little girl said, "I know, but I want someone with skin on."

There are times when we all need a friend with skin on. Sometimes we need help from others who can comfort us or, when we are ready, help us heal old beliefs.

Loving Your Wounded Child

Beliefs that cause pain can be healed (or changed) just as physical wounds can be healed. Beliefs are healed when the lie is exposed and *understanding* takes place. In her book, *Heal the Cause*, Valerie Seeman Moreton writes:

Be in Awe of the Miracle of You

When faulty programming is exposed and released, great relief is experienced. A light, open feeling of gratitude comes in and fills the empty space left by the old lie.[2]

I recently had the opportunity to test this theory and heal an old belief. I felt very intimidated by a person I admire and respect. This person was not doing anything to intimidate me. On the contrary he was very friendly and encouraging. Still I was afraid to talk with him and be friendly in return. I felt very insecure and couldn't figure out why. I tried to dismiss my thoughts and allow my natural love and security to surface, but was not successful.

I shared my dilemma with a friend who asked me to share an early memory. The one that came to me was the time I was six-years-old and my older sister was looking at herself in the mirror and said to her reflection, "You are so ugly."

I wanted to be helpful and encouraging and said, "No you aren't."

She looked at me and said, "Yes I am and you are just as ugly."

I was devastated because I loved and admired my sister. My unconscious decision was that *I'm really not good enough and people I love and respect may reject me.*

I'm not sure why this old belief affects me in some situations and doesn't in others, but I do understand that when I live from that belief I withdraw and don't allow myself to be exposed to imagined rejection. I become a six-year-old who feels very scared and insecure.

---

[2] Valerie Seeman Moreton, N.D., *Heal the Cause* (San Diego: Kalos Publishing, 1996), p. 64

My friend who was helping me suggested I picture myself as a six-year-old who was rejected by her sister and to imagine what the adult me would want to tell that child. The first thing I wanted to do was to hold her on my lap and comfort her. I imagined I would then reassure her that her sister was just in a bad mood and didn't mean what she said. I would tell her, "You are such a loving, caring, and joyful person. Everyone will always love being around you."

It was amazing that once I loved my wounded child and corrected her belief, my own beliefs were corrected. I can hardly wait to be around the person I felt intimidated by so I can give him a big hug and let him enjoy my company—as I do his.

When faulty beliefs are healed, people don't have to try to give up the misconception that they are inadequate, unloved, or can't forgive. They couldn't hang on to those beliefs if they tried. Healing takes us immediately to our hearts, where we feel love and compassion for self and others. Valerie puts it this way.

Sometimes seeing the benefit of what has happened defuses deeply held emotions even further. Seeing the benefit of the situation creates a deeper understanding of how the universe is always working to support our highest good . . . Acknowledging that benefit makes us more conscious of what is real and why forgiveness is always expedient. You can actually be happy about an uncomfortable experience when you see that a benefit has come from it. You can actually be grateful for it.[3]

---

[3] Moreton, pp. 269-270

Some may heal their beliefs by reading a book or talking with a friend. Others gain insights and inspiration in a church, through prayer, or in meditation. A personal growth seminar or therapy may be an answer for others. No matter where you seek help, be sure your goal is to overcome your programmed thought system so you can re-connect with your heart and see the perfection of all things. Gratitude will follow.

Gratitude

Having an attitude of gratitude for something that is commonly seen as very negative can be a difficult concept for some to understand. The following example may help.

At the beginning of my Positive Discipline workshops, I always ask participants what they hope to gain, knowing the workshop almost always meets all the desires mentioned. However, one woman said, "To be happy." I thought, "Hmmm. I've never heard that one before. I'm not sure that can be accomplished in this workshop."

We do a very powerful activity in this workshop where two people role-play children who receive criticism, insults, and shame from adults standing on chairs. The purpose is to demonstrate the beliefs children form (and cement into their thought systems) in response to these negative messages. One of the male adults playing a child got tears in his eyes. His pain was obvious. Some of the other participants felt very uncomfortable and thought the activity was a bit too intense. However, the man who had role-played the child said, "No. This has been extremely powerful for me. I was badly mistreated by adults when I was a child, including physical abuse. Now I feel grateful for those experiences. They have been a gift to me because I am now a child advocate who will do everything I can to prevent this from happening to other children."

At the end of the workshop, when people were sharing what they were taking away with them, the woman who had the goal of being happy said, "I learned that I can be happy no matter what has happened to me in my life."

Conclusion

We created our thought systems through a lot of self-brainwashing against ourselves. Until *understanding* becomes a permanent condition, it can be helpful to have tools for reconditioning. You may need to consciously accept yourself, no matter what, over and over again until self-love is an automatic state of being. Self-love is a natural part of your inner joy and serenity. Use your thinking ability to practice loving yourself (and your thoughts) unconditionally until it becomes automatic. And get help from *someone with skin on* when you need it.

Be in Awe of the Miracle of You

10

How Long Does it take to *Understand*?

Sometimes a deep *understanding* of these principles comes in an instant; sometimes it takes longer. For most people, *understanding* is moment to moment. They may have *understanding* at one moment and cover it up with thoughts the next. Or they may have *understanding* in certain areas and lack *understanding* in others. In either case, their feelings compass will let them know.

Many struggle as I did, knowing in my heart that the principles were true; but allowing my thought system to drive me crazy with objections and questions: "yes, but" and "how about" and "what if." Even though my thought system kept getting in the way of my understanding, my heart kept leading me back to hear more. Gradually my "yes, buts" changed to "Of course. It is so simple, so obvious, so wonderful." Before understanding, everything can seem heavy and complicated; with understanding, everything is lighter and simpler.

The learning never ends. Once you get pointed in this direction, life just keeps getting nicer and nicer. Life keeps improving even when there is complete satisfaction with the way things are.

George Pransky uses a graphic analogy to explain this phenomenon: *It is like waiting at a bus stop for the bus to deeper understanding but having such a nice time at the bus stop that you don't care if the bus comes or not.*

Glimpses Are Enough

While you are learning, it is helpful to appreciate the glimpses. Every glimpse into *understanding* is like money in the bank that you can draw on when you need it.

While writing the first edition of this book, I had a huge glimpse into the serenity and peace of mind that comes from *understanding*. I felt so loving and such joy and gratitude that it seemed that nothing could disturb my peace.

I was given a big test. I had paid a typesetter over $1,000, in advance, to complete a revision of one of my other self-published books. One day I dropped by to see how she was doing. I learned that the company had gone into some kind of bankruptcy and that someone from the court system came by every day to collect their daily receipts. Part of the bankruptcy agreement was that they had to collect a certain amount of money to hand over to the court or they would loose their business completely. So, they would work on projects for which they could collect money when they were finished—instead of projects for which the money had been received in advance and was long gone.

My friends and family could hardly believe how undisturbed I was by this news. I honestly believed that it would all turn out for the best—even if I lost the money. From this state of mind, I discussed the situation very calmly and lovingly with the woman who was working on the typesetting. I did not blame her or get angry with her. I empathized with her and the conditions under which she was working.

She stayed late and worked on her own time to finish my project. She later told me that my energy was so encouraging to her that she wanted to do all she could to help me.

I wish I could say that I was able to stay in that state of mind. I have since let other situations disturb my peace. However, that experience is *in the bank*. I love to remember it and draw on its energy as a reminder that, no matter what happens, I have a choice to deal with any situation from love or from fear.

Every time I read this book (yes, I read it over and over), it is like going to my *understanding bank*. It always takes me immediately to my heart where I experience my inherent feelings of joy and gratitude.

Glimpses are truly wonderful gifts. Be accepting of yourself while you are strengthening your *understanding* and making deposits in your *understanding bank*.

Remember that humans rarely stop thinking, even in their sleep. The point is not to stop thinking but to *understand* that thinking is a function because that *understanding* helps you dismiss illusionary thoughts so you can use your thinking ability to experience the wonders that come to you from your heart.

How Long Does it take to Understand?

Understanding frees you from the prison of your programmed thought system. A misunderstanding of the principles can lead to increased programming and misuse. I often heard comments such as the following while attending seminars to learn about the principles.

"I'm afraid to ask a question, or people will know I'm coming from my thought system instead of a higher level of consciousness."

"I still have negative thoughts, so I must not understand anything."

"I'm a failure because I yelled at my children. I lost my patience and forgot to come from my heart to see the insecurity behind their behavior."

"I really thought I understood and would not get caught up in my thought system again. The very next day I let myself get hooked into negativity, just like Pavlov's dog. I felt very discouraged and disappointed in myself."

"I just can't feel compassion when my wife drinks, or my husband yells at me, or a friend disappoints me, or things don't turn out the way I want them to. I get angry or upset."

Mistakes

Based on our level of understanding, we do the best we can; and we make mistakes on our way to deeper understanding. This is normal. Most of the people in our society have learned to accept the illusion that it is terrible to make a mistake. They equate their worth with the number or seriousness of the mistakes they make. In other words, most people have the silly thought, "If I make a mistake, there is something wrong with me."

Chapter Ten

Is it a mistake when toddlers fall down while they are learning to walk? Is it a mistake that a six year old doesn't have the vocabulary of a college graduate? Is it a mistake that a teenager doesn't have the social skills of her parents? If you make a mistake in your checkbook, does that mean you are a bad person?

With *understanding*, the concepts of *perfect* and *mistakes* are totally different. Whenever you get upset about mistakes or not being perfect, you are ego-involved. This simply means you have a belief that your self-worth is dependent on being (or having others be) a certain way. Your expectations do not allow for mistakes.

Life is full of making *mistakes*. What fun! You can appreciate your mistakes when you realize that they are simply part of your learning experiences. *You can enjoy being a rosebud until you become a rose in full bloom*

Someone once chided Thomas Edison by saying, "It is too bad you had so many failures before you were successful."

Edison replied, "I didn't have failures. I learned many things that did not work and they all gave me valuable information to finally learn what did work."

Small children have no concept of mistakes. When they fall down while learning to walk, they don't waste any time thinking about their fall. If they get hurt, they may cry for a few minutes before getting up and toddling on. Understanding the principles helps you recapture that childlike sense of wonder about mistakes as you journey through life. Mistakes will not have the conventional meaning. Instead, mistakes will hold as much joy, or interest, or wonder as all of life.

If you are still struggling, it could be because conventional wisdom about mistakes can be a tough one to give up. Let's go back to the math analogy. It is sometimes easier to understand a point when it does not involve emotions. Most of us know that making mistakes in math is not disastrous. It does not even seem like a bother to go back over the figures to find the mistakes and correct them when you feel gratitude for the knowledge allowing you to do that. Knowing how to correct mistakes is simply part of the process.

We can also use the math analogy to discuss levels of consciousness. For some of us, not knowing how to use calculus does not mean we can't use addition and subtraction to make our lives easier. The key is to have gratitude for what we do know, not to worry about what we don't know.

Although airplanes were slightly off course more than they were exactly on course (before computers), pilots did not waste time fretting but simply used their principles of navigation to keep getting back on course.

Confusion can be a good sign of progress; it may mean your thought system is being scrambled. This is a good time to dismiss your thoughts, and stop trying to figure it out, and leave room for messages from your heart. Understanding may come from your heart when you least expect it.

When you see that everything is just as it should be, you will see that creating a programmed thought system is perfect—just as an *understanding* of the thought system is perfect. The thought system can be seen as a wonderful teacher when you acknowledge how many opportunities it gives you to learn wonderful life lessons.

So remember, the four principles are like natural laws. The natural law of gravity includes no rules that you should not jump off a building; it simply explains what happens if you do. Similarly, the principle of thought as a function includes no rule that you should not think from your thought system; it simply explains what happens when you do. This information can save your life from misery, just as knowing what to do in a whirlpool can save your life literally.

Avoiding the Whirlpool Trap

When you are caught up in your thought system, it is not helpful to fight your thoughts or to try to control them. This is like trying to control a whirlpool. If you fight and struggle when you get caught in a whirlpool, it is likely that you will drown; if you relax and get very quiet, it will carry you down and spit you out at the bottom so that you can then float to the surface. However, I have a hunch that even with this knowledge, it could be difficult to relax in a whirlpool—even when the results of not relaxing could be death.

Unlike fighting a whirlpool, fighting thoughts that make you unhappy is not a life-and-death matter; it's just a matter of happiness or unhappiness. Actually, I would say that living in unhappiness is similar to living a *walking death* when a life of joy is just a dropped thought away.

It might take a huge leap of faith to relax is a whirlpool, even if you had heard of the benefits from a survivor of a whirlpool. It might take a similar leap of faith to follow suggestions from others who have used the principles to find their inner happiness. However, once you experience results yourself, you will want to relax and get quiet every time you catch yourself in your thought system.

My present level of *understanding* has increased the amount of time I live from my heart; however, it is not yet deep enough to keep me from getting hooked into my thought system at times. I would be foolish to believe the principles are invalid simply because I still get hooked at times. Instead I can feel gratitude that it is developed enough that I do not take those thoughts as seriously as I used to. I get quiet sooner. I look in the mirror sooner. I look for the lesson sooner. If I'm still stuck, I get help from someone who *understands*.

Understanding deepens as we keep listening from our hearts. As our *understanding* deepens, we find more joy and serenity in life. I am at peace knowing that *understanding* takes as long as it takes.

11

Quiet

Quiet is not necessarily an absence of action but an absence of thoughts running wild in a thought system that takes them seriously. True quiet is not always something that you *do*. It may be a feeling of serenity as you go about your daily tasks, or it may be a simple awareness of your thoughts and where they are coming from.

I remember watching a humming bird and *heard* some wisdom from my heart. "The humming bird looks *frenetic*, but it isn't. It is very *busy*, but it doesn't have stressful thoughts." That is when I realized that I could be very busy without being frenetic. The humming bird has a very quiet mind.

As I have said before, being quiet does not mean sacrificing productivity. Instead, your heart will help you be more selective in what you want to produce. You may get very busy doing what you love to do, but your mind won't be *busy* stressing. What you do will come from your joy instead of your *shoulds*.

Quiet also can be something you *do*. It has been mentioned often that getting quiet is an excellent way to dismiss the thought system, or at least to wait patiently until it loses its hold over you.

An *understanding* of the principles can lead to quiet, or quiet can lead to an *understanding* of the principles. With *understanding*, quiet is natural. Before understanding, it makes sense to actively quiet yourself by something you do, such as meditating, walking in nature, or by feeling gratitude for the many miracles in your life. Getting quiet physically may help you hear the messages from your heart.

Getting quiet can be accomplished in many ways: simply staring out the window, taking a nap, reading a book, or anything that distracts you from the busyness of your programmed thought system. Another way to get quiet is through meditation.

Meditation

Meditation can lead to the ultimate quiet for some people (going into *the silence* or *the gap between thoughts*). For others, meditation may be a time to sit quietly while being aware of their thoughts—just *watching* them. Some find it helpful to repeat a mantra over and over (such as love, peace, joy), or to say a prayer over and over such as the prayer of St. Frances of Assisi. Some meditate by counting their breaths for deep relaxation. Some meditate by chanting. Some simply sit and listen for inspiration from their hearts. In other words, there isn't a *right* way to meditate, but it can make a huge difference in your life.

For years I wanted to meditate but thought I couldn't do it. Every time I tried to meditate in groups I would either go to sleep, or my legs would twitch, or I just couldn't make my mind get quiet. It drove me crazy to sit for five minutes, let alone twenty. I just *couldn't* do it. Listen to that language; I *couldn't*? Well, it sure seemed that way.

I now meditate for at least twenty minutes almost every day. How did I get from there to here? It took commitment based on my understanding of the importance of a quiet mind to access my heart. Because of this commitment, I sat for 20 minutes a day—no matter what. I was prepared to listen to the chatter of my mind for twenty minutes if that's all that happened.

The first day I was peeking at my watch every five minutes. The second day I went fifteen minutes before I peeked. But instead of feeling energized, as I expected, I found that I was totally wiped out. So I took a nap. The third day I scheduled a walk into nature after my mediation so that I could wake up. By the fourth or fifth day, I stopped peeking at my watch and meditation began to feel wonderful.

Meditation is most effective if you leave your expectations and judgments behind. I gave up all my expectations (except for my commitment to sit for twenty minutes), and then all the expectations I had given up started to happen. Now I know that not being attached to expectations allows them room to happen—or not. And that is what my meditations are like. Sometimes I receive profound messages from my heart. Other times I simply feel love and comfort. Simply! The chatter of my mind comes and goes. I just let it be. (Well, sometimes when the chatter gets too aggravating, I may take deep breaths or concentrate on love and gratitude.)

During one of my meditations, I received the following message: *What is insight except sight from within? Walking through life without insight from your heart is like walking through life with your eyes closed.*

On my next nature walk, I tried walking with my eyes closed. Try it sometime. Find a path where there are no other people and try walking with your eyes closed. What happens? Do you feel fear, mistrust, disorientation, insecure? How long can you keep going before you feel you *have* to open your eyes? Remember, this is on a path where there are no other distractions. What happens when you try walking with your eyes closed on a busy sidewalk or on a busy street?

I realized that I am usually going through life thinking my eyes are wide open, when in truth my thoughts have created illusions that distract me from my inner peace and produce fear, mistrust, disorientation, and insecurity. When living my life from my thought system, I am literally living my life in the dark. *Understanding* the principles is like turning on the light. Quiet through mediations can facilitate the *light of understanding*.

Anyone who says they don't have time to meditate is saying they don't have time to open the eyes of their heart and soul—that they would prefer to go through life in the dark.

How much of a movie do you see when the video is on fast forward? Living your life without quiet is like keeping your life on fast-forward. You are missing the movie of your life. Pause. Get quiet. Take time for meditation and notice how much more present you will be in the joy of your own life.

Chore Meditation

You can experience a state of meditation without sitting quietly. Simply bring a state of meditation into your daily living.

Think of a chore you'd rather not do—for example, washing the dishes. Take a deep breath and quiet your mind. Then wash the dishes with love. Avoid rushing. Be fully in the moment and bring joy to every movement. Bring your gratitude to the task. It is amazing how much you can find to be grateful for: the nourishing food you ate, the wonderful invention of running water, your dishes, and your health—the fact that you are able to wash dishes. Sometimes we complain about things we *have* to do instead of feeling gratitude that we have the ability and the opportunity to do them. Slow down so you can experience gratitude instead of stress.

Nature

Quiet can be enhanced in nature. Nature feeds your soul. You need nature in your life to ground you, to nurture you, to give you messages (yes, nature will talk with you—more about that later), and to bring you to joy and gratitude.

We all love to be in nature, whether we are in a park, near the ocean, in the mountains, or near a stream, lake, or river. We feel rejuvenated and renewed in those special places (unless we are so busy in our minds that we don't even see them). When we slow down and enjoy nature, we feel relaxed and peaceful. Yet most of our time in life is spent in our busyness away from nature. In fact, some people take their busy minds with them when they go into nature and rob themselves of nature's soothing energy.

Have you forgotten about the importance of nature and how it truly feeds you to your core? Is the busyness of everyday living so important that you don't take time to feed your soul? Try taking your childlike wonder back into nature. Take time to watch it, and feel it, and enjoy it.

Many of us, and our children, have completely lost touch with the joys of nature. Many years ago, my family and I rented a camper and went to Sequoia National Park for a week. For the first two days, our children were miserable. They were devastated that they couldn't watch television. They complained that there was nothing to do. We tried to convince them that there was plenty to do in the woods, but that possibility seemed beyond their comprehension.

Eventually, however, they became bored with boredom and began to poke their heads outside. It wasn't long before they heard the call of nature. They played in the streams, climbed trees, created huts in the woods, gathered wood for the fire pit, went on hikes, played games with sticks and rocks, and chased squirrels. They were so alive. At the end of the week, they didn't want to leave.

There is an important lesson for all of us in this experience of my children. Nature is calling to all of us who are willing to listen. Our lives are enriched tremendously when we leave technology and our busy minds behind and take time to spend with nature.

Everyone can find a place to go and commune with nature. It could be a city park, the beach, the woods, the dessert, a country road—or even your back yard. Find a rock to sit on, a tree to lean on, or grass to sit on and let yourself be open to the nurturing energy of nature. Be open to messages you can receive from the wind and the sun. Ask a tree, a rock, a leaf, or any part of nature what message it has for you. Take a notepad and pencil so that you can record the message.

Chapter Eleven

I have shared this exercise with workshop participants and individuals on many occasions. Some think I must be kidding. But when they come back after doing the exercise, they are humbled. The insights they have gained and the messages they have received are truly inspiring. As they read their messages to each other, we usually have to pass the Kleenex box. People are truly moved and often see how the message someone else received is also helpful to them. You might experience personal benefit from the following message I *heard* from nature the first time I asked for a message from a tree stump.

Message from a Stump

I am a tree stump—being what I am.
I don't care about the judgments of others.
Same may say I don't have the magnificence of the
  tall, strong tree I once was.
But it doesn't matter.
Part of me was chopped down and hauled away
  for some good use, I am sure.
I am still beautiful.
Look at my patterns—in my bark, in my bare wood,
  in the niches and crevices where bugs find refuge.
You may stand on me, or sit on me and bask in the sun.
My message to you about love: There is nothing to be
  except who you are.
Look closely and see the beauty of who you are.

You might enjoy keeping a nature messages journal. Write down the messages you receive from different parts of nature. One day it may be a tree. Another day it may be a leaf, a raindrop, a twig, a pond, a mountain, sand, or a rock. The possibilities are endless—as are the messages.

Spiritual Messages Everywhere

Spiritual messages can also be found in everything that happens to you. For example, on my walk one morning I was listening to some music on my small tape player. The earphones started to buzz. I wondered what the spiritual message could be, but it quickly became so obvious: *Your mind is buzzing away all the time. Don't let it interfere. Just let it be and enjoy the music. You don't have to make your thoughts go away. Just don't give them so much energy and other information will get through.* An amazing thing happened. The buzzing in the earphones stopped. Another amazing thing happened. My buzzing thoughts didn't stop. I'm joking, of course—it's not at all amazing that my thoughts kept buzzing. They never stop, but how nice to know that I don't have to pay so much attention to them. When we are open to spiritual messages, they can be found anytime we are willing to receive them.

Let's tackle a seemingly difficult situation. Suppose someone you love leaves you. What kind of spiritual message could there possibly be in that? Could it be that there is something better in store for you—perhaps a better relationship or an occasion to learn how much you can enjoy being by yourself, or an opportunity to enjoy your friends. Could it be that your heart and soul know that it is not good for you to be with this person?

We have all heard stories about people who believed that being abandoned by their spouses was the worst thing that could ever happen to them, until time passed (sometimes years) and they came to see that their spouses leaving was the best thing that could have happened to them.

We can't hear spiritual messages when we give more credibility to our egos and programmed beliefs than we do to our hearts. And that is okay. We are ready when we are ready. If you aren't ready to see spiritual messages in so called catastrophic events, start with less emotional events. Suppose you are taking a walk and you come to a big hill. You are tired and *think* you can't make it. Tune in to the message from the hill. The first question you may hear is, "Do you really *want* to climb this hill?" Maybe it is time to turn around and go in another direction. If you do want to climb the hill, you may get other messages, such as "Slow down. What's the hurry?" Take time to rest. Go one step at a time. Pause and look at the beautiful scenery all around you." Another message could be that the difficult climb will strengthen your muscles and help you become more fit. Then comes the fun part. Notice how all those messages may fit perfectly in your life. Focus on a life problem you are having. See if any of the messages would be helpful.

Quieting your mind and ego (dismissing your thought system) creates openness to many unusual and joyful possibilities. In her book, *A Return to Love*, Marianne Williamson confirms what happens when we forget that we created our thought systems and egos.

Not everyone chooses to heed the call of his own heart. As all of us are only too aware, the loud and frantic voices of the outer world easily drown out the small still loving voice within.[1]

Many of us who seek quiet use the ego of our thought system to defeat ourselves in many ways. Four ways to consider are expectations, self-defeating judgments, lack of awareness, and not seeing the gift in all things.

Expectations

George had a great meditation. He felt connected to his soul. He felt love and joy. The energy was so strong that he walked around in bliss for a day. The next morning he meditated and was very disappointed. His experience was nothing like the day before. He spent the rest of that day in total depression. What had happened?

George's expectations got in the way. He wanted his second meditation to be just like the first. George wasn't aware of it, but his expectations had become part of his programmed thought system—a great barrier that can keep him from his heart and soul.

Self-Defeating Judgments

Then George allowed his judgments to take over. He beat up on himself for not having a *high enough* level of consciousness to meditate *right*. He compared himself to others who surely had better meditation experiences than he did—all the time.

---

[1] Marianne Williamson, *A Return to Love* (New York: Harper Paperbacks, 1992), p.35

Chapter Eleven

Lack of Awareness

Of course, George wasn't aware that it was his expectations and judgments that were creating blocks. If he had been aware of this, he could have dismissed them to be more open to his heart—without attachment to the outcome. Judgments and expectations can't take over unless we let them. We let them take over when we forget that they don't have a life of their own—we create them. Awareness leads to *understanding*, or *understanding* leads to awareness. We can then be open to seeing the gifts in whatever happens.

Not Seeing the Gift in All Things

George had heard about seeing the gift in all things. The third day he sat in mediation and asked his heart to show him the gift in what he was experiencing. He soon received an insight about his expectations and his judgments and he chuckled. He then realized how often he let his expectations and judgments keep him from seeing the gifts in his life experiences. He still did not have the same experience as his meditation on the first day every time, but he stopped comparing them. He felt total joy in what he did experience.

Another message that came to him was, *What is, IS.* He had heard that before, but now it had new meaning for him. He knew that on same days he may not receive any messages at all but that sitting quietly during his meditation time would be enough—a beautiful gift. When he felt blocked, he would tune into the blocks and see if they had anything to teach him.

He began to feel gratitude for all of it: his thought system, his ego, the four principles that taught him to *play* with his thoughts instead of taking them seriously, and the life lessons he learned. Most of all, he felt gratitude for the understanding that helps him connect with his heart whenever he chooses.

Quiet is the humility you feel in the absence of troubling thoughts and beliefs. In a quiet and humble state of mind, you will have a different experience of life. The world looks very different when seen through your natural feelings of love, gratitude, and compassion—for yourself and others.

Enjoy quiet.

12

Contrary to Popular Opinion

C onventional thinking is very different from heart wisdom. One of the beliefs perpetuated by conventional thinking is that you can *give* self-esteem to another person.

Self-Esteem

Have you noticed that self-esteem (as defined by the world) is very elusive? One minute you have it and the next you don't—depending on what you do or what others think. When you do something well or someone praises you, you feel good and experience self-esteem. However, when you don't do well or when someone criticizes you, your self-esteem disappears.

Contrary to Popular Opinion

Wayne Dyer tells a story about a woman who believed she was inadequate because her husband said she was. She complained, "He gives me an inferiority complex.

Wayne wondered jokingly, "How did he give you an inferiority complex? Is this something he purchased at a store so he could give it to you as a gift?"

The woman just looked confused, so Wayne continued, "If your husband said you were a car, would that make you a car?"

She replied, "Of course not."

Wayne persisted, "Wait a minute. What if he tried to put gas in your ear; then would you believe you are a car?"

She laughed, "No, I'm not a car."

Wayne concluded, "Then why would you believe you are inadequate? Obviously he can't make you believe anything you choose not to believe."

This woman's inferiority complex did not come from her husband's criticism but from *her thoughts about* them. If she would dismiss her thoughts about her husband's comments, from her heart she would know that what he says comes from his separate reality. She would see the innocence and insecurity behind what he is saying.

With *understanding,* she would know what to do. Instead of taking his thoughts seriously, she might feel inspired to hug him, make a joke, take a walk, leave him, or whatever her inner wisdom would lead to her to do. Have you ever noticed that people don't use intimidation with people who don't get hooked by it? When she stops getting hooked, her husband may stop. If he doesn't, her inner wisdom can lead her to the next step.

Self-esteem from the thought system is a moment-to moment state of mind. When you are listening to your heart and inner wisdom, you have natural self-esteem. When you are dependant on the approval of others, you don't. Self-esteem is one of the natural good feelings inherent in every human being. Permanent self-esteem is a heart matter, not a head matter.

Rules

As your *understanding* deepens, you will realize that when living from your heart, you do not need rules. Rules are like *shoulds,* with a sense of punishment and reward attached. Principles are natural laws, which help you understand the natural consequences of what you do.

Many rules are based on fear. Some people fear that without rules, anarchy will prevail—rape, murder, lying, cheating, and stealing. This is not true. Most people would not consider these acts even if there were no laws against them. And people who perform these acts are not stopped by laws. People enjoying their inner wisdom do positive things naturally—without rules.

It makes no sense to rely on rules when you have access to your inner wisdom and inspiration. As your heart guides you through each day, you will experience positive results and enjoy life. On the other hand, what happens when you rely on rules? The rule becomes more important than the intent of the rule. The *spirit* of the law becomes the *letter* of the law and usually invites rebellion or guilt and blind obedience. The joy of doing what is *right,* because it feels good, is lost.

The thought system invites all kinds of *mischief.* Some use rules to make judgments against others (who aren't obeying the rules to their satisfaction), or they use the rules against themselves—judging themselves for not obeying the rules well enough. Self judgments create depression and insecurity, and more rule breaking, and more self-judgment: a vicious cycle. From the heart, people do what makes sense in loving and respectful ways.

Although the four principles may sound like rules, they are not. A principle is like a road map: it does not include rules about where you *should* go but lets you know where you are or where you will end up, depending on which direction you travel. If you are in Virginia and want to go to New York, it makes no sense to go south. The four principles let you know that if you are feeling bad and want to feel good, it makes no sense to use your thought system and take your negative thoughts seriously.

By turning any of the examples or suggestions in this book into rules, you make them part of your thought system—changing them beyond recognition of your inner wisdom. They are no longer principles.

Decisions

Contrary to popular opinion, it is not helpful to figure things out or make decisions when you are upset. This only keeps you deeply enmeshed in your thought system and is as ineffective as keeping your foot on the gas pedal to get out of a ditch while the spinning wheel digs deeper and deeper into the sand.

If you have any doubts about what to do, or if you want to do something because of negative feelings such as anger, let that be your clue that you are lost in your thought system. Get quiet and wait for your negative feelings to pass so your inner wisdom can surface. You will know decisions are inspiration from your heart when they produce peaceful results. You will not doubt their appropriateness even if you hear a contrary message from your thought system.

Chapter Twelve

Actually, the concept of decision making changes with an understanding of the four principles. The familiar concept of decision making implies choice or effort. With *understanding*, decisions feel more like obvious, commonsense things to do. Deepak Chopra discusses this as *The Law of Least Effort*, the fourth of *The Seven Spiritual Laws of Success:*

> *Least effort is expended when your actions are motivated by love, because nature is held together by the energy of love. When you seek power and control over other people, you waste energy. When you seek money or power for the sake of the ego, you spend energy chasing the illusion of happiness instead of enjoying happiness in the moment. When you seek money for personal gain only, you cut off the flow of energy to yourself, and interfere with the expression of nature's intelligence. But when your actions are motivated by love, there is no waste of energy. When your actions are motivated by love, your energy multiplies and accumulates—and the surplus energy you gather and enjoy can be channeled to create anything that you want, including unlimited wealth.*[1]

Recently, I was trying to make a decision about how to handle a situation where I felt treated unjustly by someone. I thought I had made some progress because of my willingness to take responsibility for how I had helped create the situation. I knew that I was still in my thought system, however, because I wanted to confront this person, tell him how I felt, and let him know I was

---

[1] Deepak Chopra, *The Seven Laws of Spiritual Success* (San Rafael: Amber-Allen Publishing & New World Library, 1994)

going to make sure I did not invite unjust treatment anymore. This decision did not create good feelings.

I decided to get quiet and meditate for a while. It didn't take long for me to receive a message: *Are you going to use love power or anger power? Sharing your feelings from love will be much more effective than sharing them from anger. There will be no sense of blame. You will simply practice what you know about identifying a problem and finding a solution. Taking responsibility is much more effective from love than from anger.*

Once again, I saw how easy it is to make rules out of wisdom. I had seen the wisdom of taking responsibility for how I contribute to situations. In this situation, I was doing this as a rule and it didn't help me feel better. As soon as I used my feelings compass to find that I was in my thought system, I was open for fresh inspiration from my heart.

When I talked with my friend, I was able to state the problem without negative emotions. I simply said, "This is a problem, and I know we can find a solution." And we did because he did not feel defensive, as he most likely would have if I had attacked him.

It is easy to turn a successful decision into a rule. However, a decision may make sense in one situation, but not in another. No matter how similar the situation is, it may call for a completely different decision at another time or for someone else. Only your inner wisdom can let you know.

Idleness is the Devil's Workshop

Many of us have been taught that *idleness is the devil's workshop.* The truth is that *quiet is the heart's workshop.* Quiet allows you to be open for inspiration. Nevertheless, so many people fear that if they are not constantly busy, they will not be productive.

146

Chapter Twelve

Productivity from inspiration produces happiness; productivity from the thought system produces unhappiness. We may be productive in achievement, material prosperity, or a spotless house while our personal family life is falling apart. Or we may be productive trying to find satisfaction outside ourselves and wonder why we never feel satisfied.

Again, it is never *what* we do that matters but rather why we do it and how we feel as we achieve our results. When we are idle because we are happy and want to just enjoy life, we will find more happiness. When we are idle because we are unhappy, depressed, or bored, our discontent grows worse.

There is a popular opinion today that watching television is a waste of time. Maybe so, maybe not. We may watch television as part of our enjoyment of life, or as an effort to escape life. We may avoid watching television because we are afraid of what other people will think or because we have adopted the notion that only uneducated people who don't have anything better to do watch television.

The same could be said of any activity or inactivity in life. When achieving happiness and peace of mind is your only goal, you will know what to do regardless of what anyone else has ever thought or said.

Doing

What you do depends on your state of mind. When you allow your natural good feelings to surface, what you do from this happy state of mind will be different from what you do in a state of mind created by your thought system.

Let me give you an example. When you are *nice* because you think that is how you *should* behave, there will be a nagging dissatisfaction. Often there are strings attached—expectations such as "If I'm nice, then things should turn out my way," or, "Then people will love me." The world looks and feels different when you are *nice* because it feels like the natural thing to do. You will experience satisfaction and contentment. There are no strings attached. There is true joy in the doing.

Sometimes you may feel inspired to do something nice, but your thoughts sneak in and turn it into a *should*. You will know this has happened when your feelings change from peaceful to stressful, anxious, or resentful. A friend shared how this had happened to her. She loved baking cookies for friends and family during the holidays, but one year she realized it was no longer fun because she felt that she should bake cookies for what had become a long list of people. What she had started from her heart crossed over to her thought system and the joy was gone.

We live in a speeded up world. There is so much *doing* going on and not enough *being*. The ego of the thought system thrives in a busy world. Heart wisdom thrives in a quiet world. Your inner wisdom is always with you, but you can't listen to it if you don't slow down. I want to stress again that slowing down does not mean you have to be bored or non-productive, as illustrated in the following fairy tale.

A Fairy Tale of Two Princesses

Once upon a time there two princesses: Princess Dew and Princess Bee. Princess Dew was very busy running around doing things for other people, trying to make them happy. Some people loved what Princess Dew did for them, but instead of being happy, they just wanted more. Princess Dew tried hard to do more for them, hoping that someday they would be happy. Other people did not like what she did for them *for their own good* and wished she would stop interfering.

Princess Dew became worn-out, bitter, and frustrated because people did not appreciate all she did for them. She was very unhappy. No one wanted to be around her.

Princess Bee was also very busy—being happy. She enjoyed just about everything: rainbows and clouds, rainy days and sunny days. She especially enjoyed people. She loved watching them *be*. People loved being around her. Her happiness was contagious.

Service

The fairy tale of Princess Bee and Princess Dew is not meant to suggest that we should not do things for others. A happy state of mind will probably inspire you to be of service to others in any way you can. What you do, however, will not come from *shoulds* or ulterior motives, and it will not be conditional. Service will be for the joy of the moment.

You will also know when to be of service to yourself. Taking care of yourself is not selfish when it is inspired from your heart. *The greatest thing you can do for yourself and your relationships is to take care of yourself and be happy.*

Selfishness

It is popular to have strong negative opinions about selfishness, and, it fact, the self-centeredness that comes from the thought system looks and feels like the popular definitions of selfishness. The self-interest that comes from the heart and a happy state of mind, however, has a different look and feel.

The difference is in the foundation. Selfishness from the thought system is based on ego, self-importance, resentment, rebellion, or total disregard for others—all based on the illusion of insecurity. Self-interest from the heart is based on feelings of love and the joy of living. With these feelings, you will want to do whatever your inner wisdom leads you to do to enjoy life.

Because of your old beliefs about selfishness, you could let your thought system convince you that doing what you want to do is *selfish*. If you stick to following the feelings from you heart, however, you will know the difference no matter what anyone else thinks.

One day Mary felt like going for a nice, long walk. She received a message from her thought system: "You should not go for a walk when you have so many other things to do, like cleaning the house and grocery shopping." She dismissed her thoughts and listened to her heart. She went for a walk and enjoyed the beautiful day. Her family came home to a happy wife and mother. They enjoyed being around her and felt her love.

Martha also wanted to go for a walk, but she listened to the *should*s from her thought system. She felt depressed and did not get much cleaning done. Her family came home to an unhappy wife and mother.

If you are asking, "How will anything ever get done if we always do what we want instead of doing what really needs to be done?" you have missed the point. The next day Martha went for a walk but still felt depressed because she felt guilty. Mary stayed home and cleaned the house and still felt happy.

From a happy feeling, Mary is able to know what is important for her own well-being and that of her family. From an unhappy feeling, Martha will feel dissatisfied no matter what she does. For example, Martha has trouble getting her children to do their chores, while Mary has inspiration for how to win the cooperation of her children. When Mary cleans house, it is because she enjoys a clean house, not because she is compulsive or following *shoulds*. When Martha cleans the house, she is trying to prove that she is a good wife and mother. However, just the fact that she thinks she needs to prove she is a good wife, means she doesn't believe she is; so she will never be able to prove it.

In your heart, you know there is nothing to prove. That is a function of the thought system. When you enjoy a nice life living from your heart, you will be creating serenity in your home and in the world. Happiness and peace of mind are contagious.

The Road to Hell is Paved with Good Intentions

Knowing that people have good intentions can inspire compassion instead of judgments. When good intentions fail, it is usually because thought-produced insecurities create detours.

We all have good intentions to be happy and do the best we can based on our present level of understanding. People who commit the most heinous crimes truly "know not what they do." They are deeply entrenched in a programmed thought system where *understanding* is beyond their reality.

Forgiveness is easy when we understand the good intentions of ourselves and others; it is difficult when we pay attention to the behavior resulting from the insecurities produced by a distorted thought system.

People locked into their thought system and negative behaviors create a kind of hell for themselves. It is our judgments of them that lead to our own kind of hell. Understanding that everyone has good intentions may set you free.

A Person without Goals Is Like a Ship without a Rudder

In some cases, a person with goals may be like a boat, not without a rudder but with a rudder stuck in one position. Being without goals allows us to enjoy opportunities as they come along.

I know I'm getting repetitious, but again—the secret is from whence the goals come. Goals from the heart will be much different from goals of the thought system.

New Year's resolutions so often fail after a brief spurt of success because it can take too much energy to satisfy the ego. So, we give up. Success is effortless, however, when following inspiration from the heart.

Deepak Chopra describes the difference between coming from the thought system or the heart when he writes:

> *Learn to harness the power of intention, and you can create anything you desire. You can still get results through effort and through trying, but at a cost. The cost is stress, heart attacks, and the compromised function of your immune system.*[2]

We often look at someone who is accomplishing something and say, "Wow, she really has self-discipline and sticks to her goals." If you take a closer look, you may find that she is following not a goal but inspiration. Inspiration provides energy, whereas goals from the thought system drain energy. It is difficult not to follow inspiration, but it can be difficult to muster the energy to pursue goals from other sources. The goals you set from your heart

---

[2] Deepak Chopra, *The Seven Laws of Spiritual Success* (San Rafael, CA: Amber-Allen Publishing & New World Library, 1994) pp. 75-76.

and soul will be filled with passion. Achieving them will be pure joy work rather than pressure and dread work.

Anything worth Doing is worth Doing Well

The maxim "Anything worth doing is worth doing well" may be true if *well* simply means that you enjoy doing it, but *well* is usually a judgment, with implications of perfection. Beliefs about perfection often take the joy out of doing.

How many people will not sing for the fun of it because they feel that they cannot sing well enough? This is just one example of the many things people avoid doing for pleasure because they're afraid they won't live up to the judgment of doing it *well*. Anything worth doing is worth doing for the fun of it!

Suggestions

It doesn't matter if you choose not to follow any of the suggestions proposed in this book; their only purpose is to help you see the principles. If you don't see the wisdom behind the suggestions, they will appear to be just more *rules* and *shoulds* and will only create more insecurity, burdens, arguments, or other dissatisfaction. If a suggestion doesn't inspire insight from your inner wisdom, just forget about it and keep listening from your heart and you will receive inspiration when you least expect it.

Suggestions about what to *do* will be meaningful only if you feel confirmation in your heart. When you feel the truth in your heart, the suggestions may trigger your own insights and life lessons.

Heart confirmation means that you have captured the feeling of the principle rather than the words. Follow the wisdom of your heart and you'll know exactly what to do. Your inherent good feelings will guide you to eliminate stress and to find serenity in your life and your relationships.

13

Detours

There are many detours that can keep you from accessing your innate natural good feelings. For example, it is easy to go down the *big A* detour when your thought system is in control.

Anger

You may get angry when people don't drive the way you want them to or when others don't respond as you want them to at exactly the moment you want them to (preferably by reading your mind). You may get angry when equipment doesn't work the way you want it to or when a retail clerk doesn't behave as though you are the most important customer in the store. You get angry about standing in lines (why are all these other people here?).You may get especially angry when someone else gets angry at you. I'm sure you could add to this list.

When people see their anger as reality, they have different ways of expressing it. Sometimes they verbalize their anger, sometimes they sulk, and sometimes they have a silent tantrum against themselves and get depressed. They miss so much of the beauty of life when they take this detour.

Another common detour is the belief that there are certain things that justify anger. It is normal to feel angry when you perceive that you have been violated in any way. However, maintained anger over this or any other immoral act does not solve anything; it just makes you feel bad and keeps you from enjoying life *now* or from accessing your inner wisdom to know what to do.

Christine Heath, a therapist with the Hawaii Counseling and Education Center, and the Minneapolis Counseling and Education Center, worked in group-therapy sessions with sixty women who were victims of rape or incest. For many years these women talked about their anger, beat on pillows, and yelled and screamed about their anger. They spent hours confirming that what had happened to them in the past was the reason they could not hold jobs, were alcoholics, and could not have lasting relationships.

After Christine learned about the four principles, she apologized to the women in her groups: "I'm sorry, but I have been doing it all wrong. From now on we will no longer dwell on the past but will talk about some principles that will teach you how to have happiness and peace of mind now."

A few women dropped out because they did not what to give up their anger. The remaining women soon learned to enjoy life when they stopped living in the past through their thought systems. A two-year follow-up showed that they maintained their good feelings and were successful in their jobs and relationships. Some were training to become therapists or educators so they could share what they had learned with others.

One woman appeared on a panel with other rape victims. She was obviously a very happy person. The moderator of the panel questioned her, "Don't you feel angry? Hasn't your rape experience affected your relationships with men? Why are you so happy?

"That experience took up eleven minutes of my life," she answered. "I don't intend to give it one more second in my thoughts. Life is so full of good things to enjoy, why should I waste time thinking about the past?"

When you don't like what happened in the past, it doesn't make sense to keep re-creating it in your thoughts and then multiplying the unhappiness by adding anger.

There is a popular opinion that if you don't get your anger out, you will store it and it will fester. This can be true when you are living from your thought system. Stored anger based on past perceptions and beliefs can fester into physical disease, and it can destroy relationships. Biofeedback research suggests that one moment of thought-provoked anger substantially suppressed the immune system for eight hours. Other research demonstrates the healing effectiveness of the natural good feelings from the heart.

Obviously, it is not a good idea to store anger. The key is *how* to get it out. One way is to *understand* the thinking ability that created the thoughts that led to anger and then dismiss them. Another way is to share how you feel (not how some one else has *made* you feel) in a way that invites clarification of separate realities. What you do is not as important as the state of mind behind what you do. Sharing how you feel from your heart is very different from sharing your feelings from your thought system.

Another way to get anger out (literally) is to look for the lesson, or gift. Your anger could have a very important life message for you. Anger turns into resentment when you miss the message but keep the messenger. We have already discussed how *looking in the mirror* for reflections of yourself can lead to *understanding.* Try methods for getting quiet discussed in chapter 11. Like all negative thoughts, anger loses its power when seen with *understanding.*

Love transforms anger. The heart sees innocence. The heart feels compassion. The heart *understands.* Healing beliefs from the past can be so complete that decisions from the past are gone.

More about the Past

The past can be a popular detour unless awareness of past beliefs leads to dismissing them or to the healing of unconscious beliefs.

Through brain research, it has been discovered that our brains are storage containers for every thing in our pasts. Wilder Penfield[1] found that he could probe any part of the brain and the patient would remember the details of specific events from the past, including smells and feelings:

> *When Penfield considered his results, it appeared that the brain held an untold number of film clips, each with sound and picture, of vivid events from the patient's past. The*

---

[1] Jefferson Lewis, *Something Hidden: A biography of Wilder Penfiled* (Garden City, New York: Doubleday & Company, Inc., 1981), p. 201

replaying would evoke, as well, the emotions that accompanied the original experiences.[2]

The brain also stores our interpretations of past events even though they are not correct. The thought system turns these interpretations into beliefs that act as filters to keep us from seeing the truth in the moment. We stay in the present when living from our hearts.

So even though the brain stores everything from the past, it takes a thought system to interpret these events. The past cannot exist unless we think about it, yet many live their whole lives on this detour. Valerie Seeman Moreton teaches:

Sometimes it takes a healing process to expose the subconscious thought or belief behind anger, hurt, or any other debilitating emotion. An important part of healing is "walking in another person's shoes"... Go into that persons' head to understand and identify their thoughts and feelings and intentions,[3]

A healing process can help an individual truly understand separate realities with compassion and forgiveness. The first time Valerie led me through her healing process (which she calls the Kalos Process), she did muscle testing to determine when I decided I wasn't good enough. (She just assumed I had made this decision because it is such a universal conclusion of most

---

[2] Lewis, p. 198.

[3] Valerie Seeman Moreton, N.D., *Heal the Cause* (San Diego: Kalos Publishing, 1996) p. 339

children.) I tested strong (my upheld arm had strength) when she asked, "Was it at the age of two?"

Valerie then asked, "What happened when you were two?"

I didn't have a clue, so she asked me to make something up. I knew that anything I made up would be part of my subconscious so I *made up* the following memory and was surprised at how real it felt to me.

"I'm two-years-old and my father is bouncing my six-month-old baby brother on his knee. I'm wondering why he doesn't bounce me on his knee. I'm deciding it is because I'm not good enough."

Valerie said, "Let's check it out. Are you willing to get into the head of your father, knowing he can not do you any harm and you can't do him any harm?" (Kalos is an eyes closed process that takes place during a state of deep relaxation.)

I agreed.

Valerie then talked to me as though I was my father and asked, "What do you see in front of you?"

My father (through me) replied, "A cute little boy that I'm bouncing on my knee, and an adorable little girl with curly blond hair."

Valerie: "Do you love this little girl?"

My father: "Of course I love her."

Valerie, "Why don't you bounce her on your knee?"

My father, "You don't bounce girls. They are too delicate."

Valerie, "Can you tell her that you love her?"

My father, "I'm not sure why, but I feel very uncomfortable saying that. Maybe it is because I never heard my parents say it."

My father did not have to go any further. Suddenly I felt complete understanding, compassion, and forgiveness. I had spent years dealing with my belief that my father didn't love me, which must mean I wasn't good enough, which must mean I needed to prove I'm good enough, which never worked. Now I could no longer *get away* with those false illusions. I knew beyond a doubt that my father had loved me and had shown it in the very best way he could (the way his parents had shown love to him), with lots of lectures, pointing out mistakes in a misguided attempt to motivate improvement, and with no physical or verbal displays of affection. Compassion and love were not just words for me. These feelings were profound. I also knew that it would not have mattered even if my father didn't love me. That would have been about him, not me.

As in the above example, you may have decided you were unlovable or inadequate during your childhood. This decision was not made based on the truth. Your parents may have reprimanded you because they believed that was the best way to show their love. They may have been too busy *doing* to give you the attention you wanted. The truth did not matter as much as your *interpretation* of the situation, which was cemented into a belief. This belief may act as a filter to keep you from accepting love in the present. *Understanding* can eliminate the belief. When you *see* and interpret an event differently, from your heart, your feelings and decisions will also change.

Insecurity

Even though insecurity is just another thought, it can be very powerful when taken seriously. Most of the problems we create for ourselves are based on the illusion of insecurity. In other words, if someone says or does something that hurts you, it is because of his or her insecurity. The fact that you feel hurt is due to your own insecurity. Why would you feel hurt about what someone else says or does unless your thought system is taking his or her thoughts seriously?

Thought-provoked insecurity (whether conscious on subconscious) may appear in the form of aggressiveness, shyness, drug-abuse, self-righteousness, selfishness, feelings of inadequacy, the need to prove self-worth through achievements, or any other *misbehavior* designed to over-compensate for the illusion of insecurity. Temporary relief might be found through achievements or other forms of compensation, but it doesn't last. From your heart, you won't judge these behaviors; you will *understand.*

Illusionary insecurity may lead you to adopt the belief systems of others or to imagine that others are the source of your self-worth. It is easy to see how this occurs when we are small. We want so much to be loved and to belong. We don't know any better than to listen to our parents, who too often are coming from their thought systems.

The teen years often present a vulnerable time because adolescents want so much to *fit in.* And when teenagers cave in to peer-pressure, they relinquish their ability to listen to their inner wisdom. What a difference it could make for them to *understand* the four principles.

Many positive behaviors also are motivated by insecurity from the thought system. *Pleasers (approval junkies)* do loving things for others to *buy* love. Power mongers may engage in positive actions to serve their purposes. (I won't even go into politics.) Talk about interesting.

Chapter Thirteen

Ego and Self-Importance

The illusion of insecurity is strongly connected to the ego's need for self-importance—an impossible route to happiness and serenity. When you get off track into your thought system, notice how often the detour is related to proving your self. It can be overwhelming just to think about all the antics we go through in life to prove something that has no need to be proven.

The ego is the strongest part of the thought system. It works very hard to protect itself. It is not at all interested in being dismissed and replaced by your heart. However, you will feel like a different person when you don't take your ego seriously. Your worth (or the worth of anyone) is not an issue when you see yourself and others from your heart.

I used to scoff at the question "Who am I?" Now the question makes sense because I realize I am different when experiencing life through my heart than I am when experiencing life through my thought system and ego. I know that my spirit or soul is perfect and incapable of anything but love and joy. I also know that I'm involved in some perfect plan that involves the creation of a thought system and ego to provide lessons that my soul could not learn in any other way.

Meanwhile, I experience my natural happiness when I recognize my ego for what it is and stop taking it seriously. Then I know I have nothing to prove. Instead I can enjoy *being.*

The fun thing about the ego is that every time you recognize it for what it is, you can't help laughing about the mischief it creates, thus causing it to lose its power. Your ego loves catching you off guard, however, so that it can sneak back and take charge. By keeping the principles in mind, you can play hide-and-seek with your ego.

It Is Easy To See In Others

Have you ever noticed how easy it is to observe illusionary beliefs in others and how difficult it is to maintain that perspective with yourself? The thought systems and egos of characters in movies and novels become very obvious when observed through an *understanding* of the four principles. Life can be a joy when you have as much fun catching your own ego and observing you own thought system—without judgment.

Righteous Judgments

Many who take the judgment detour excuse their judgment of others by calling it *righteous* judgment. Righteous judgment is rare; because it is based on feelings of love and understanding. It leaves no negative feelings in its wake. Instead, the results of righteous judgment can be positive. Abhorring child abuse is an example of righteous judgment when it is followed by actions to protect children and educate parents out of love and compassion instead of self-righteousness.

"I'm telling you this for your own good," is not an example of righteous judgment but of taking your own separate reality seriously and thinking it is the *right* reality. Self-righteous judgment of others is not helpful; it leaves negative feelings. When you dismiss your thought system, you rise to a higher level of consciousness where judgments are replaced with love, compassion, and inspiration.

In his lectures, Wayne Dryer often gives the analogy of an orange to make the point that what we see comes from inside us.

Chapter Thirteen

When you squeeze an orange, you get orange juice because that is what is inside the orange. When humans get "squeezed" (challenged), what they see in others can be seen only if it is inside them. *If you look closely, you will always find the trait inside you (when coming from your thought system) that you are judging in another.* Of course, you won't think your trait is as bad. Thinking that someone else is "worse" is a vain attempt to justify your own behavior. Rudolf Dreikurs called this *deflating another in order to inflate oneself.* Others have given the example of three fingers pointing back at you whenever you point a finger at someone else. From your heart all judgments disappear and you see the world through your natural good feelings. What a difference!

Stereotyping

Another danger of judgment is that we often characterize people by what they do from their thought systems and decide that this is the sum total of who they are. Often we dismiss what they do from their hearts as *just an act.* We are more willing to trust the validity of behavior from a low mood than behavior from a high mood. This is mischievous behavior from the ego trying to convince us that thought system behavior is more real than heart behavior.

Your thought system often may react negatively to the thought system behavior of others. Your heart will know that this is when people need compassion rather than judgment.

Judgments from others

With *understanding,* you will pay no more attention to the judgments of others than to your own. You will see that you get into enough trouble taking your own thoughts seriously. *Shoulds* and *shouldn'ts* are no more helpful from others than they are from yourself.

Virginia dreaded being around her mother for long because she felt intimidated by her mother's judgments. Virginia reacted to these judgments with rebellion. Her mother reacted to Virginia's rebellion with more judgments. So, round and round they would go.

After learning about the principles, Virginia spent a delightful four days traveling across the country with her mother. As Virginia tells the story, "Every time my mom voiced an opinion that I used to call judgment, I just saw it as her reality. Instead of rebelling and letting her know that I thought what she thought was stupid, I saw it as interesting. I could even see the insecurity behind her so-called judgments and felt compassion for her. I still didn't agree with her on everything, but I respected her right to see things differently. I was able to respect my own way of seeing things without getting huffy about it. We had a great time. We talked and shared more than we have in my whole life."

Living For—or Against Someone Else

Too many people take the detour of trying to live up to the expectations of others and become *pleasers*, or *approval junkies*. By doing so, they discount their own heart and inner wisdom. Others take the detour of rebelling against the expectations of others, even when following their suggestions might be to their benefit. It is easy to understand why and how people create these decisions when we look at their childhood conditioning and understand the need to live up to the expectations of parents and teachers or to rebel against them.

Once there was a little girl named Marie who went to visit her aunt and uncle where she learned to bake bread. Her aunt and uncle thought she was wonderful and praised her and told her over and over how much they appreciated her bread.

Marie went home and baked bread for her family. No one said anything about her bread. They just ate it. Marie decided she would never make bread for her family again because they didn't appreciate it and praise her.

Then one day she discovered that she enjoyed making bread for the fun of it. She loved getting her hands into the dough to knead it; she loved the aroma of the baking bread; and she especially loved eating it hot out of the oven, dripping with butter and sometimes honey. She also loved sharing it with anyone who wanted to have some. She realized that when she was living *for* or *against* someone else, she didn't taste the bread.

Perception Prisons

Hanging on to false perceptions is another detour and will keep you from you natural happiness. It is important to remember that all negative reactions are based on thoughts and false perceptions. As the *Course in Miracles* teaches us in lesson 5, "I am never upset for the reason I think"[4] Lesson 7 teaches, "I see only the past."[5] This is an excellent description of the thought system. Everything we see from our thought system is seen through the filters of our past. When we do not *understand* these perception prisons, we are

---

[4] *A Course in Miracles: Workbook for Students* (Huntington Station, New York: The Foundation for Inner peace) p. 8
[5] Ibid p. 11

blocked from our ability to see with fresh perspective from our inner wisdom.

Three sisters got together at a family reunion and began discussing the past. Each had perceptions of events that had a profound impact on the decisions they had made about themselves. However, when each shared her memory, the other two sisters were surprised at the interpretation. All of them had been present at each event, yet each had experienced them very differently. Which perception of each memory was *the truth?* The past is not the truth. The past is only your perception of the truth.

When you understand that the past exists only when you think about it and that it is only your interpretation of what happened, it becomes difficult to take your thoughts about the past seriously. In the same way, when you see the innocence of others, knowing that they did the best they could from their level of understanding at the time, you will feel different about those actions.

Paula often complained about all the terrible things her mother had done and said to her in the past. A therapist asked her, "Do you think your mother stayed up late at night plotting ways to make your life miserable?"

With reluctance, Paula admitted, "No."

A week later Paula said that question helped her understand the principles of separate realities and led her out of her thought system to her heart where she felt compassion and forgiveness. It had become clear to her that her mother really did love her and had done the best she could, considering her own insecurities.

Paula added that her inner wisdom then led her to "look in the mirror" and see how she was repeating many of the same behaviors with her own son: "I punish him when he makes mistakes, even though I hated it when my mother did that. I can see now that she probably did it for the same reason I do. I'm afraid that if I don't punish him, he won't learn to do better, and I want him to do better because I love him. But when I was a child, I can remember wishing my mother would understand how I felt and teach me with love instead of punishment."

Paula was able to forgive her mother and herself when she understood that the *mistakes* they had both made were simply the results of getting sidetracked from love and enjoyment of their children into the thoughts that produced fear and insecurity.

Lighten Up, Keep It Simple, and Come From Love

When you lighten up and quit taking things too seriously, what once seemed like a tragedy can be seen as an interesting event, as a stepping-stone rather than a stumbling block, as a great gift full of lessons to be learned, or simply as a humorous situation.

Keeping it simple usually means that the solution becomes obvious and uncomplicated when you drop your judgments that lead to anger, hatred, revenge, or self-pity. Trying to figure things out from your thought system is usually complicated. Figuring things out from your heart is simple.

When you are coming from your heart, you will know that what you do is not as important as how you do it. For example, maybe it would be a wise thing to fire an employee or leave a relationship. These things can be done with love and respect rather than with anger and revenge. When you are doing what needs to be done to handle situations, there is no need for anger. Just about everything can be done with love.

It Gets Easier To Avoid Detours

Even a limited understanding of the principles keeps you pointed in the right direction so that your understanding keeps getting deeper. The deeper the understanding, the easier it gets to avoid detours. Let good feelings from your heart be your guide to avoid detours, to enjoy the detours, or to find your way back home.

14

Relationships

There are many different kinds of relationships: Spouses, children, parents, friends, animals, colleagues, bosses, employees, and drivers on the freeway. Some are closer than others. Have you noticed that those closest to you often trigger the ego of your thought system easier than any other kind of relationship? Have you noticed how much easier it can be to share wisdom with friends who are having relationship problems than to see wisdom for yourself when you become emotionally involved?

My sister will point it out to me when I do or say something to my husband that sounds disrespectful to her. I'm usually surprised—either because I hadn't even realized what I was doing, or I felt *justified* and she just didn't understand. Then she will do or say something similar to her husband and I'm appalled at how awful it sounds.

Why is that? Why is it sometimes easier to have empathy and show more respect for others than it is to those closest to us? And why is it sometimes easier to give unconditional love to an animal than to a person?

The last question provides the best analogy—animals don't challenge your thought system or your ego. You probably don't have unrealistic expectations of your pets. You don't get upset when an animal doesn't *agree* with you. And, you experience unconditional love from your pets. They are very forgiving.

I'm not suggesting that you treat those you love like animals (although I considered it) but to use this analogy as another way to help you understand the power of the thought system to cause problems. The four principles can show you where problems originate in any relationship. They can show you why those closest to you can be the most challenging to your thought system. Let's take a look at how the four principles affect relationships.

Separate Realities Relating To Relationships

Have you even tried to convince your partner (or child) that your point of view was the right one and felt as if you were talking to a wall? Actually you were talking to two walls: the wall of your own unique reality and the wall of your partner's unique reality. (Talking to a wall could be easier because a wall does not have its own point of view and you wouldn't have any expectations from a wall.)

Chapter Fourteen

It is not productive to try convincing your partner, who already knows how things are and would like to you convince you. Your partner is usually seeing his or her own reality with as much inner wisdom as you are seeing yours: zero.

Amy and Sean had daily arguments. No matter what the subject, the theme was always the same.

Amy: "You have to be blind as a bat not to see things my way!"

Sean: "If you had any brains at all, you would know that *my* way is right!"

Amy and Sean are stuck in the illusion of their separate realities.

Jeannette strongly believed her children needed lots of rules and guidance. Duane believed he should sacrifice anything important to him in order to cater to their whims. Duane thought Jeannette was a tyrant. Jeannette thought Duane was a wimp. Both were so entrenched in their separate realities that they did not have access to their inner wisdom.

Jeannette and Duane found a therapist who taught them about the four principles. It was interesting that they both received the same message from their inner wisdom when they dismissed their thought systems. "Maybe we are both taking an extreme position and could learn a lot from each other when sharing from our hearts." The guidance and inspiration they received from their hearts was very different from their former positions based on self-righteous, defensiveness, and judgments. When they quit taking their separate realities seriously they found that their heart realities were very similar.

Dorene and Charles were experiencing marital difficulty because they were deeply enmeshed in their separate realities. Their distorted frames of reference prevented them from seeing anything with love and compassion.

Dorene complained about being third or fourth priority in Charles's life. From this belief, she felt hurt. As many of us do, she covered her hurt feelings with anger, which she expressed by blaming and attacking Charles for not putting her first.

Charles took her attacks seriously and experienced feelings of inadequacy and defensiveness, which he expressed by acting disdainful towards Doreen. Charles's frame of reference included a belief that women were unfair and unreasonable anyway.

During her childhood, Doreen had an experience that she interpreted to mean that she was unimportant. She turned this interpretation into a belief that distorted every experience she had from then on. Subconsciously, she spent her life looking for evidence to support her belief in her unimportance. She was so intent on this task that she missed any evidence that might change her belief.

This was obvious when she told the story of how she and Charles met and got married. Charles was dating Adele but quit seeing her and soon asked Doreen to marry him. Doreen did not see this as evidence that she was important to Charles. What she did notice was Adele's name on the wedding invitation list, which she saw as evidence that Adele was more important to him than she was. Charles's attempts to explain that he simply liked Adele as a friend fell on deaf ears.

Charles, in turn, had a childhood experience that he had interpreted to mean that women were unfair and unreasonable. He adopted this as such a strong belief that he was unaware of how he set women up to prove that he was right. In this case, he knew Doreen would probably be upset if he put Adele's name on the list. Even though it wasn't important to have Adele as a wedding guest, he wanted to be able to prove he was right about how unreasonable women can be. Of course, neither was consciously aware of the childhood beliefs that created the filters in their thought systems.

You and I have enough perspective (because we are removed) to see the humor in the emotions and dramas they created by their thinking, but Doreen and Charles were not laughing. They were focused on what they were looking for through the filters of their thought systems, which left little time to share good feelings and wisdom from their hearts. They were so focused on looking for evidence to support their distorted beliefs that they missed the obvious, wonderful things going on around them.

We can always create what we are looking for. For example, if we believe that we will be rejected, we will act in such a way that invites rejection, or we will see rejection even in innocent behaviors.

After hearing about the four principles, Doreen and Charles finally dismissed their thoughts and saw each other very differently. They stopped *playing detective* (looking for evidence to support their insecurities), and started seeing each other from their hearts instead of their heads. Charles felt like reassuring Doreen that she was important, and Doreen felt like reassuring Charles that she trusted him. Neither one really needed reassurance anymore, but each appreciated the loving gestures. They had learned to laugh at their silly thoughts and see the beauty of life and of each other.

Acceptance

A marriage counselor suggested to Hazel that she stop trying to change her husband and accept him the way he was. Three months later, Hazel complained, "But I *have* accepted him for three whole months, and he hasn't changed a bit!" It is obvious that Hazel did not accept her husband the way he was, but thought that conditional acceptance would motivate him to change.

Acceptance means respecting differences, not conditional acceptance while expecting changes. Even though it is impossible to change other people's realities (only they can do that by changing their own thoughts), we often keep trying. *True acceptance is unconditional and allows us to see others with compassion, gratitude, and love.*

Chapter Fourteen

Thoughts and Moods Relating To Relationships

Mary thought that Jim was not paying enough attention to her. When she self-righteously shared this with her friends, they told her the importance of letting him know how she felt. Mary decided that was a good idea. That night when Jim sat down on the couch and started to read the newspaper, she sat next to him and said, "How come the newspaper is more important to you than I am?

Jim defensively retorted, "Because the newspaper doesn't hassle me."

Mary ran to the bedroom and cried. For the rest of the evening she did not speak to Jim. The next day she told all of her friends that Jim had admitted he preferred the newspaper over her, so she might as well get a divorce.

Before filing for divorce, Mary had an opportunity to learn about the principles. As a result, she dismissed the notions of insecurity from her thought system and was amazed how her feelings about herself and Jim changed when she saw the world from her heart. She knew what to do.

The next time Jim sat down to read the newspaper, she sat quietly next to him, feeling gratitude for having such a nice man for a husband. She could see past his defensive behavior and felt unconditional love for Jim because she had dismissed her own insecurities, judgments, and expectations.

Soon Jim put down the newspaper and gruffly asked, "Did you want to talk?" Mary could feel that he was still in a low mood and replied, "No, I was just enjoying your company." Suspiciously, Jim continued to read the newspaper. For several weeks, Mary continued to enjoy just being with Jim, no matter what he did. She had discovered her own inner happiness and peace of mind and was not affected by outside circumstances.

One day Jim came into the kitchen while Mary was preparing dinner. She asked, "Did you want something?" "No," he replied, "I just wanted to be with you."

Some people who hear this story think Mary acted like a wimp who decided to passively put up with a jerk. But look at her results: She found serenity, saw the goodness beneath Jim's gruffness, and inspired him to experience his own heart. Unconditional love has the power to lead others to their heart center when they are ready.

Another person might follow his or her wisdom to do something else. When living from the heart, there are infinite possibilities about what to do, but the feelings behind the doing will be the same: compassion, forgiveness, gratitude, and all the other feelings that are the essence of love.

We reap what we sow: When we put negativity out into the world, we get negativity back. Yet when negativity comes back, most people forget that they put it out in the first place. They don't take responsibility for their part it its creation. (Mary did not see that she helped create Jim's defensive actions and gruffness with her expectations and criticism.) In the same way, when we put love out into the world, love comes back. Joy and happiness are contagious.

Are you still thinking that sometimes negative circumstances come to you even when you did nothing to create them? The point is that even if you have no personal responsibility for causing certain events, you do have responsibility for your *thoughts about them.* As you know by now, your thoughts can give you more trouble than the circumstances themselves.

Sue's husband had an affair and she was so hurt that she wanted revenge. She went to an attorney and said, "I want to hurt him as much as he hurt me. I want to leave him with as little as possible financially and to limit his child visitation rights. I will make sure the kids don't even want to see him."

Sue was too hurt and angry to see that it was her thoughts about this situation that made her miserable. Fortunately, she chose a wise attorney, who asked, "Do you really want to hurt him in the worst way possible?"

"Yes."

The attorney said, "Then go back and live with him for six months. Be the very best wife you can imagine. Be loving, compassionate, understanding, forgiving, affectionate, and fun. He will feel lucky and will start loving you very much. In six months you can start the divorce proceedings and he will feel extremely hurt emotionally and financially."

Sue objected, "I couldn't stand to live with him for six more months after what he did."

"Well, then you must not really want to hurt him in the worst way possible."

"Oh, yes I do," Sue said. "I will do it."

Two years later, the attorney saw Sue walking down a street. He asked, "What happened? I thought you were going to come back for a divorce."

Sue replied, "Are you kidding? He is the most wonderful man in the world. I wouldn't even think of leaving him." She must have done such a good job acting loving that she soon forgot it was an act and started enjoying the good feelings. Good feelings are extremely contagious, creating more good feelings in people who come in contact with them. People do change in an atmosphere of unconditional love.

When an *understanding* of the principles changes how you see things, everything and everyone in your world looks different. It may seem as though others have changed, but it is your thoughts, and thus your reality and your feelings that have changed. Others respond to your feeling level. When you give love, you get love—not necessarily because others give it back to you but because love will emanate from within. Feeling love does not depend on anything or anyone else.

You may ask, "But what if I just don't feel loving, and I'm not willing to *act* as Sue did?" Whenever you feel the need to ask what to do, it is helpful to do nothing except dismiss your thoughts, get quiet, and wait until you know what to do from your inner wisdom. You may feel inspired to do something very different from what Sue did.

And if you don't feel ready, you don't feel ready. What is, *Is*. To simply accept *what is* can be very calming.

Listening

Understanding the four principles changes the experience of listening. True listening is forgetting about the details, hearing what another person is feeling, and knowing when those feelings are coming from thoughts of insecurity. You recognize the difference from your own feeling level. When you feel love, compassion, or interest rather than judgment or defensiveness, you listen deeply.

When your partner is upset or caught up in his or her thought system, that is the time to listen, not to talk. Analyzing does not help. Listening is quietly responding with love. When you are in that state of mind you will receive inspiration to let you know exactly how to express love and encouragement eventually, if not immediately. It might be humor. It might be time alone. It might be a loving touch. It might be a quiet walk. It might be time to rest. It might be time for reflective listening. You will know.

Another way for couples to avoid low moods is to avoid the thought system by just having fun together.

Have Fun Together

Have you ever noticed that when you are having fun together, you are not being judgmental, critical, or dissatisfied? Having fun can act as a catalyst to take you out of your thought system. When you want to experience love and good feelings in your relationships, it makes sense to do things together that bring pleasure and enjoyment.

Live In Gratitude

When you dismiss negative thoughts, you are left with feelings of gratitude and appreciation for all that your relationships have to offer. It makes no sense to live in negativity when love is just dropped thought away. When following the treasure map to happiness and peace of mind, the natural state of a relationship is to enjoy unconditional love.

Relationships

15

Myths about Relationships

Y ou will find that reality, as seen through your heart and inner wisdom, is often quite different from what you may have been taught all your life about relationships.

Myth No. 1: Love is Blind

Love from the heart is not blind. However, love from the thought system can be very blind. Too often people *fall in love* with their *fantasy* of another person—what they *think* the other person is rather than who he or she really is. They are too busy seeing someone through the filters of their personal insecurities and fantasies to see the person heart to heart. When the fantasy doesn't live up to their expectations people think their *love was blind* instead of realizing their thought systems were blind.

Because of the Universal Law of Attraction, you will attract people into your life with the same level of energy vibration. If you think you are insecure, you will attract people who will give you lots of opportunity to verify what you believe. On the other hand, if you are filled with love and joy, you will attract others who are filled with love and joy.

Does this mean you and the others you attract into your life will be perfect? Yes and no. When you believe in the perfection of all things—everything is perfect. As the Course in Miracles teaches, every encounter is a holy encounter. Everyone has something to teach you about yourself. If perfection means never making mistakes or never getting caught up in your thought system, then no, you and others aren't perfect. However you will see mistakes as nothing more than opportunities to learn. So called *faults* provide information for improvement (after unconditional acceptance).

When you love another person heart to heart, you are not blinded by judgments, insecurities, expectations, and fantasies. You see differences as interesting or with understanding and compassion. This is unconditional love. It is when the thought system kicks in that the trouble starts.

Because Bob promised to call Nancy at 9:30 but didn't call until 11:00, she thought he was inconsiderate and uncaring—and told him so. Her feelings let her know that she was in her thought system and this *understanding* immediately took her to her heart. She remembered that when they were experiencing heart to heart love she had been understanding and compassionate when Bob called later than he had promised. It became obvious to her that it wasn't the circumstances but her thoughts that upset her. Her judgments and anger were her defense mechanisms to cover up feelings of insecurity. From her heart, she felt secure and loving again. She expressed delight whenever Bob called. Bob felt like calling more often.

The judgment blinder is so powerful that it can even change what was once seen as a virtue into a *fault*. Marilyn fell in love with Jordan and admired the calm way he drove a car, which made her feel safe and relaxed. After they got married, however, she found that it often drove her crazy to ride with him because he was not aggressive enough and didn't take risks to pass slow cars.

Marilyn had also admired Jordan for his quiet, easy-going dependability; he had been in the same job for twelve years, and she could set her clock by his departure and arrival. With her judgment glasses on, however, she started seeing him as boring and lacking in ambition. During their courtship, she had loved his flexibility and willingness to go along with all her suggestions. But through her judgment blinders, she saw him as spineless and weak, without an original thought in his head.

Marilyn divorced Jordan and married Steve, who was aggressive, ambitious, and opinionated. At first Marilyn admired these *virtues* in Steve and felt lucky to be married to an exciting man who knew what he wanted and where he was going. She felt protected and taken care of. Later, however, she saw him as controlling and unyielding because he would not do what she wanted him to do. Instead of feeling protected, she felt dominated and not taken seriously.

Marilyn divorced Steve and married another man like Jordan. She is now in her seventh marriage because she does not see that she loses her good feelings and happiness every time she goes into her thought system and sees the world through her judgments and expectations. She believes she sees reality through her thought system. Also, she is looking for happiness outsider herself and blames others when she doesn't find it there.

Myth No. 2: It Is Important To Be Compatible

Dolores divorced Scott. Her explanation: "We just weren't compatible." A pervasive distortion of the meaning of compatibility is the notion that two people must be *the same* to live together harmoniously.

When you understand the principle of separate realities, you can see that it is impossible for two people to be the same. Even couples fooled into thinking they have the same interests and beliefs get into trouble when they later discover that what they thought was the same is not.

Dolores and Scott were delighted to discover that they both enjoyed tennis. They were already *in love* but saw their mutual interest in tennis as proof they were *compatible*. The trouble started because Dolores liked to play more often than Scott did, and he thought she took it too seriously. Dolores assumed that anyone really interested in tennis would feel exactly the same way she did. Both felt cheated and misunderstood. Since they were apparently not as compatible as they had thought, divorce was the only solution they could see.

The true meaning of compatibility is having the ability to love unconditionally. We all have this ability because compatibility is a natural state when we dismiss negative thoughts and respect differences instead of judging them. We have compatibility when we see differences with interest, respect, and love.

Chapter Fifteen

Myth No. 3 It Is Important To Communicate About Problems

An overemphasis on the importance of communication in relationships is another pervasive distortion. How often have you heard someone say, "We just can't communicate," or, "The key to a good relationship is communication"?

The distortion in these statements is the implied importance of making your partner understand and accept what you feel and what you believe. That is, if you can get your partner to believe your reality rather than his or her own, you have succeeded in *good* communication. This is the same as saying, "You should have my illusions, not your own."

No wonder so many are failing in their attempts at communication. It is impossible for your partner to believe your reality rather than his or her own. With *understanding,* you both might dismiss your realities for the thought created illusions that they are. Until then you may prefer to *fight rather than switch.*

Because you are always communicating, either from your distorted thought system (fear) or from your heart (love), it is important to know where your communication is coming from. Even sulky or angry silences are a form of communication. When you are communicating from your heart, however, you are sharing the positive feelings that you experience through love, wisdom and inspiration.

When you are in a state of happiness and peace of mind, it is amazing how much you can enjoy what is usually referred to as mundane information. "Is dinner ready?" "I paid the bills today." "How are the kids?" "Shall we go to the beach?" Communication becomes light and easy, not heavy as it is when you communicate to "get it all out" or to make sure your partner knows how you feel—from your thought system.

This may sound boring to some people, but happiness and peace of mind are never boring. In a happy state of mind it is common to feel so full of the joy of living and love for your partner that you are filled with gratitude.

You may wonder, "Does this mean we shouldn't talk about our separate realities?" What you do is not the point. Talking about your separate realities, or not talking about them, is simply a different experience when you understand the principles. It is not what you *do* that is important but rather the *feeling* behind what you do. With *understanding,* you will probably feel a sense of humor or respectful interest if you do talk about separate realities.

Myth No. 4: Never Go TO Sleep Until You Have Resolved an Argument

Sometimes the best way to dismiss thoughts of right and wrong is to agree in advance to some kind of cooling-off period to help you get quiet. This could be done by sleeping it off, walking around the block, or doing sometime else that helps you feel better.

Kate and Frank believed that they should never go to sleep until they had resolved their arguments. They would stand toe to toe and argue about who was right and who was wrong. Since they were both caught up in their individual thought systems and separate realities, it was impossible to hear each other or solve anything. Since they believed they should be able to solve their arguments, their frustrations would build. Frank would finally leave, slamming the door behind him and go to the nearest bar. Kate would go to bed but couldn't sleep because she was furiously thinking about their failure to solve the problem before going to sleep.

When they saw a therapist who taught them about the principles, they saw how they could agree in advance to get quiet when they got caught up in their thought systems. Frank said to Kate, "Since I like to leave the house when I am upset. I will leave, but I won't slam the door, and I won't go to a bar. I'll take a walk around the block until my thought system is tucked away where it can't hurt me and I am able to enjoy how much I love you again. You can know that my leaving is not anger at you but just my recognition that I'm caught up in my thoughts and need to get quiet until they go away."

Kate said, "Since I enjoy relaxing in bed, I will do that. But instead of continuing to think about my negative thoughts, I will read a book or go to sleep with the reassuring knowledge that they are just thoughts. You can know I'm not going to bed to get away from you but to rest until the negative thoughts are gone and nothing is left but love."

Myth No. 5: A relationship without fights is superficial or One-Sided

Couples who understand the principles do not fight, or at least they realize that they are off track when they do. The peace between them does not mean that they are not going *deep enough* in their relationship or that one of them is surrendering too much. On the contrary, they respect each other instead of their programmed thought systems.

"Lisa and I still have fights," said Scott, "but they are all silent. We know that if we feel like fighting, we are just in a low mood or lost in our thought systems, so we keep quiet and wait for it to pass."

Beth said, "Tom and I used to have fights and lose respect for each other. We still have fights once in awhile, but now we lose respect for the fights instead of for each other."

"When Dave and I have fights now," said Kathie, "we seldom take them seriously for long, so we end up laughing. It is especially fun to watch my 'Sarah Bernhardt act' while I am still taking things a little bit seriously."

I used to get upset when I wanted to *discuss* something with my husband, and he would tell me, "Forget it." I would think, "What do you mean, 'forget it'? If you had any sensitivity at all, you would be upset too." Now I say, "Thanks for reminding me."

Myth No. 6: You'll be Happy Once Circumstances Change

Happiness is a state of mind that has nothing to do with circumstances. "Dear Abby" received a letter from a women complaining about her husband's snoring. In reply, "Dear Abby" quoted a letter from another woman: "I used to complain about snoring. My husband is dead now. I would give anything to be able to hear him snoring again."

An often-told story is the one about struggling newlyweds who do not appreciate the joy of being together and in love because they keep focusing on how much better it will be when they have more money, a house, and furniture. Then they get the money, house, and furniture but don't enjoy them because they think they are not as much in love as they used to be. In fact, they do not experience the joy of love because they keep focusing on circumstances. They cannot see what *is* when focusing on what *is not.* In our thought systems, we want more, better, different. In our hearts, we feel contentment and gratitude. We experience joy in our relationships when we love unconditionally.

June was miserable because her husband, Cy, was an alcoholic. She vowed to herself that if he did not stop drinking by the time the children left home, she would leave him. They had been married thirty years when the last child left for college. Before June kept her vow, she decided to see a therapist who taught her the principles. She decided to try meditation to see if she could receive a message about what to do. She was surprised at the clear inspiration she received from her inner wisdom: "It is not your province to judge your husband but to love him unconditionally." June's reality changed; she loved Cy unconditionally without effort, and within three months he stopped drinking.

Some people have interpreted this story to mean that a person should deny the problems of alcoholism and become an *enabler* by ignoring the issue. If you have heard the principles with *understanding,* you realize that the story does not set forth a rule; it simply tells what happened to one woman who listened to the inspiration from her inner wisdom. Someone else might hear a totally different message. The message could be to leave with love or to lovingly insist on an intervention program. The possibilities are limitless. Only one thing will always be the same: positive results are experienced when following your inner wisdom.

Myth No. 7: Jealousy is a Sign of Caring

Jealousy is created from the ego and is based on the notion that possessiveness will cure feelings of inadequacy. It is a way of trying to get someone else to take responsibility for your own happiness.

Myths About Relationships

Bill and Sue went to a party. When he saw her dancing with another man, he became angry. He sulked on the way home until Sue persuaded him to admit that something was wrong. Then he blew up! He blamed her for flirting and accused her of being inconsiderate. He would not accept her explanation that she didn't especially want to dance with the other man but didn't know how to refuse gracefully.

Bill had become so lost in the contents of his thinking that he didn't connect his behavior with thoughts of insecurity. He had used blame to cover up his fear that Sue might find him inadequate compared to the other man and that she might decide to reject him—a fear against which he felt powerless. Expressing anger gave him a false sense of power and control, but certainly not happiness.

Bill decided to leave Sue to protect himself from being left by her. He created the very thing he feared in order to protect himself from what he feared. The thought system can inspire some very crazy thinking and actions.

It is easy for us to see the absurdity when observing the illusions of others. *Understanding* helps us see the absurdity of our own illusions with compassion.

Jealousy, which is based on an illusionary feeling of unimportance, is just another form of insecurity that takes many forms. Many people base their lives on these illusions, wasting time and energy trying to hide their fears or trying to blame themselves or others as the cause of their fears.

Fears of inadequacy take such forms as "I won't be good enough. Someone else will be better than I am. If only I were more beautiful (or handsome, powerful, successful, intelligent, witty) then I would be okay."

Fears of rejection take such forms as "He won't care as much as I care, which means I'm not good enough, so he might leave me, and then I'll be alone and will never find anyone else."

Fears of powerlessness take such forms as "I can't do anything about this. I have no control over what is happening to me. I can't make someone love me."

All these fears are self-worth issues. The belief that anyone can lack self-worth is an illusion based on years of conditioning from childhood. When we *understand* this, we can have compassion for ourselves for buying into the illusions and compassion for those who perpetuated it out of their lack of *understanding.* Before *understanding,* however, the illusions created by the thought system are powerful detours away from happiness in relationships.

Myth No. 8: You Must Have a Relationship

Who said you must have a relationship? This is just another belief based on another thought. When you look at the evidence, it makes no sense. There are just as many (or more) *un*happy people in relationships as there are happy people in relationships, and there are people who are happy without a relationship as well as unhappy people in the same circumstance. You can be in love with life alone as well as with someone.

Again, it's not the circumstances themselves but how you think about them. When you have peace of mind, gratitude, and satisfaction with all that *is,* you don't see what is not. You are happy with or without a relationship.

Myths About Relationships

16

Keys to Happiness:
A Summary

Would you like to be in prison? Would you knowingly confine yourself to a life sentence in a dungeon? These questions may sound ridiculous, but your thought system can create a prison as confining as any dungeon. The prison walls you create in your mind are formed from illusionary thoughts, but they can be as binding as concrete.

The foundation stones for this prison are made of thoughts that create feelings of insecurity. The walls are made of whatever form the insecurity takes: drinking, anxiety, overeating, judgment, overachievement, expectations, stress, dissatisfaction, depression, blame, concern about what others think. The ceiling is the belief that these thoughts are reality.

The Four Principles as Keys to Happiness

An *understanding* of the four principles discussed in previous chapters is the master key to the prison doors. *Know the truth and the truth will set you free.*

Deep within you know the truth of these statements. However, there can be a wide chasm between intellectual knowledge and experiential reality. Intellectually, I believed that happiness came from within, but I did not understand the barriers that kept me from experiencing this truth. An *understanding* of the four principles provided the treasure map that led me past the barriers to my inner happiness. This chapter provides a brief summary.

Thinking as a Function

The foundation principle is realizing that *thinking is a function.* This realization is the key to experiencing natural mental health and inner happiness. Those who believe wholly in the contents of their thinking often experience stress, anxiety, and other forms of insecurity. They take their thoughts seriously, turn them into beliefs, and live for them. They have created perception prisons.

Those who *understand* that thinking is a function experience freedom and their natural state of being—love, wisdom, gratitude, compassion, joy. *Understanding* helps you see the humor in your thought creations so you can enjoy those that serve you and dismiss those that don't. Your prison doors will be unlocked.

Feelings as a compass

The principle of *using your feelings as a compass* is the tool that lets you know where you are on your treasure map. When you are experiencing negative feelings, you have forgotten that thinking is a function, and therefore you are seeing your thoughts as reality. Anytime you are feeling unconditional love, joy, gratitude, or compassion, the treasure is no longer buried; you are living from your heart and inner wisdom.

Separate Realities

When you understand the principle of *separate realities,* you see differences with interest and compassion rather than with judgment. Compassion does not mean you approve of every action by others; it means you understand their insecurity and lack of *understanding.* You stop making yourself miserable through judgments. You understand that s*erenity is just a dropped thought away.*

Mood Levels

The principle of *mood levels,* or *levels of consciousness,* is closely related to the others. You are in a low mood or level of consciousness when you forget that thinking is a function, when you forget to respect separate realities, when you forget to use your feelings compass as a guide, and especially when you try to use your thought system to find a solution to your predicament. Persistent low moods may be giving you the message that you need to seek help to heal thoughts and beliefs from your deeply programmed thought system. An *understanding* of this principle can lead you to compassion for yourself while you wait for a low mood to pass. An *understanding* of the following barriers to happiness can help.

Circumstances

It is never the circumstances but your thoughts about them that create your state of mind. Refusing to *understand* this truth is what keeps people imprisoned in hopelessness, victim mentally, or the bitterness of hanging on to grievances instead of forgiving. One key to happiness is to look for the gifts in your circumstances.

A good example is the story of two men who lost their fortunes. One was distraught about his circumstances and jumped off a tall building. The other man saw the same circumstances as an opportunity to start over again in something new. As you might expect, the man who jumped off the building was not a happy person even when he had his fortune; whereas the man who saw the opportunity had been enjoying life during all his varied circumstances.

Some argue, "I can understand how this applies to most circumstances, but not to others." People will often think of extreme cases to prove a principle invalid instead of simply applying the principles to circumstances where they know it is true.

I have found that as I experience the principles in areas where I do not doubt, my understanding deepens. I then doubt less and see the principles in areas I had formerly been unable to understand. This is a progression that never ends.

When you are confronted with circumstances that you can't seem to understand and you add negative thoughts to them, you have two things to make you miserable: the circumstances and your negative thoughts about them. Your thoughts are usually much worse than the circumstances, and it is your thoughts that produce your feelings.

You may ask, "But what if I'm not in a state of mind that allows me to see things without judgment? What if I do have negative thoughts and feelings about external circumstances?"

The most helpful thing is to accept yourself and have compassion for yourself as you are—without judgment. Of course this can be difficult because when your state of mind comes from your thought system, it is difficult to have compassion even for yourself. This is why it can be helpful to get quiet and just wait for it to pass. Knowledge of the four principles may help you do at least that much. Knowing it will pass, even when you feel stuck, is the first step toward getting unstuck. *Understanding* keeps deepening, and life keeps appearing more beautiful.

Judgments

You judge others when you forget about separate realities and delude yourself into thinking that your reality is the right one. For every thing or every one you judge, someone else has been able to see the same event or person with compassion and understanding. Judgment is similar to the pot calling the kettle black or *looking for the mote in the eye of another, when the beam in your own eye distorts your view.*

Keys to Happiness: A Summary

When you observe others through your judgment filters, you are defining your own state of mind while believing you are defining theirs. The person you are judging may be blinded by insecurity or some other form of negativity; but if you were not blinded by the filters of your thought system, you would see the innocence and realize that person just doesn't know better. Instead of judging, you might then be inspired to do something to help that person feel more secure, or, you might know that the best thing to do is to get out of his or her way.

It may help you get past your judgments by using the *mirror insight process*. What *fault* of your own is reflected in your judgments? The prison doors open when you see your own faults mirrored in others and have compassion for yourself as well as them. You can then seek the wisdom of your heart to heal the *fault* or just dismiss the thought and let it go.

Expectations

When you are focused on expectations, you can be blind to the beauty and wonders right in front of you. A key to happiness is to give up your expectations so you can see and enjoy *what Is.* Remember; there are miracles all around you in every moment. When living life from your heart, you *see* the miracles and are filled with gratitude.

Beliefs and Realities

Alfred Adler once said, "Ideas have no meaning expect the meaning we give them." We often attach such importance to the meaning we assign to our thoughts and ideas that they become beliefs we live and die for.

A firm belief in the flatness of the world does not make it so. A key to happiness is remembering that beliefs and realities are creations of your thoughts. Most of your thoughts were programmed when you couldn't see the truth, just as you can't see that the world is round. The truth that you find in your heart and inner wisdom can free you from the beliefs you created as a child.

Gratitude

Joe: "I can't see anything to be grateful for in this messed-up world."

Wise old Zeke: "I'll bet you would be a millionaire if I gave you $100 for everything you could think of to be grateful for."

You will see what you look for. It is impossible to feel gratitude and negativity at the same time. Your *understanding* of this truth will let you know that it makes sense to focus on what you are grateful for rather than on what you have been thinking about to make yourself unhappy.

Gratitude is my favorite key to happiness.

Compassion

Feeling compassion is another natural state of being that bobs to the top when you dismiss your thoughts. With perspective, you see the innocence in others and know that they do the very best they can from their present level of understanding.

A key to happiness is allowing yourself to experience the compassion from your heart that makes it easy to forgive yourself and others.

Keys to Happiness: A Summary

Forgiveness

An unwillingness to forgive is one of the greatest blocks to inner wisdom. *Forgiveness is natural from a level of consciousness that includes compassion, love, humor, gratitude, and peace of mind.*

The ego has some very powerful hooks. Being "right" is a huge one. For many of us, being right wins over love and peace too often. Being right can take many forms. Sometimes we feel that we have a *right* to feel miserable. After all, look what those people (our parents) or that person (boss, spouse, friend, relative) did to us. I would much rather feel miserable about that than to let it go and feel love and peace. That would mean I would have to let go of all my judgments and feel compassion—and (gulp) even forgive." There is only one thing to be gained by not forgiving—misery!

People who have the popular opinion that forgiveness is something they have to work at, or try to do, are engrossed in ego and judgment. It is self-righteous to think, "Well, I know you did something wrong, but I will be big enough to forgive you." Or, "You did a despicable thing and you don't deserve forgiveness." Lack of forgiveness harms the unforgiving more than the unforgiven. It is impossible to be happy while holding on to judgments.

Anyone who says, "I will forgive, but I won't forget," doesn't *understand* forgiveness. Forgiveness *is* forgetting. It is realizing that ego, expectations, and judgments are thoughts that are not worth hanging on to. When we let go of them, they are forgotten. When you see people or situations with *understanding,* there is nothing to forgive. You see their innocence when you realize that they truly *"know not what they do"* when coming from their thought systems instead of their hearts. Dismissing programmed thoughts and forgiving are synonymous.

Forgiveness is natural from a level of consciousness that includes compassion, love, humor, gratitude, and peace of mind. Forgiveness is not even an issue when we have these feelings because when we see with *understanding,* there is nothing to forgive.

The Battle between Love and Ego

Love is the ultimate reality; ego is the ultimate illusion. Ego is the need to prove self-importance based on the illusionary belief in insecurity. It is the source of jealousy, self-righteousness, possessiveness, judgment, expectations, revenge, depression, stress, and disease. What power this illusion of ego can create.

But love has a greater power. Love heals every problem. Through the perspective of love, problems disappear. Love fills us with inspiration that guides us to solutions that make the problem seem insignificant.

Joe chided to Zeke, "All this talk of love sounds like religion and the flower children of the sixties to me. It really turns me off."

Wise old Zeke replied, "Could it be that the reason you don't have much love in your life is because it turns you off?"

A key to happiness is recognizing the difference between love and ego so that ego can be dismissed and love can be enjoyed.

Enjoying what *Is* while it *Is*

Have you ever looked back at a time in your life and thought, "I was really happy then. Too bad I didn't appreciate it more at the time?" Have you known others who thought that their circumstances were a tragedy but later saw them as the best thing that ever happened to them? These are examples of the perfection in all things.

When you *understand* the principles, the beauty of life is profound. What used to seem ordinary or insignificant is seen with appreciation and gratitude. You will be so filled with beauty, contentment, and the wonder of life that you will have no choice except to get quiet and enjoy it. A key to happiness is to enjoy what is.

Love and Understanding

The greatest key of all is love. When you feel loving, you see beauty and goodness in everything—or at least, you see the perfection of all things.

Love and *understanding* are the same. Love without understanding is conditional (not love at all). With *understanding* it is impossible to judge; with *understanding* you have compassion; with *understanding* you have peace of mind and contentment; with *understanding* you have love.

Remember that *understanding* is not about *shoulds*. Suppose you don't feel loving? No problem. You feel what you feel based on your present level of understanding. *Shoulding* on yourself just makes it worse. *Understanding* usually changes what you feel, but if you try to change it through *shoulds*, you block *understanding*.

A key to happiness is listening to your inner wisdom until *understanding* sneaks past your thought system.

Happiness and Serenity

What could be more important than happiness and serenity? When happiness is what you want, it makes no sense to entertain thoughts that lead in any other direction.

Chapter Sixteen

Can you imagine the wonderful revolution that will take place when we all start dismissing the many thoughts that create so much misery? This key to happiness is simple. Dismiss negative thoughts and you have happiness and serenity.

As a man thinketh, so is he. What thoughts are you willing to give up your happiness for?

Keys to Happiness: A Summary

References

Chapter One

Deepak Chopra, *The Seven Laws of Spiritual Success* (San Rafael: Amber-Allen Publishing & New World Library, 1994), pp. 43-44.

David R. Hawkins, *Power VS. Force: The Hidden Determinants of Human Behavior* (Carlsbad, CA: Hay House, Inc., 2002), p. 246

Chapter Two

Wayne Dyer, *Secrets of the Universe*, Nightingale Conant Corp., The Human Resources Company, Chicago, IL

Chopra, Deepak, *The Book of Secrets: Unlocking the Hidden Dimensions of Your Life,* Random House, New York, NY 2004

Sue Pettit, *Coming Home*, available from The WV Initiative for Innate Health, Robert C Byrd Health Sciences Center, 1 Medical Center Drive, PO Box 9147, Morgantown, WV 26506-9147

Rick Suarez, Ph.D, and Roger C. Mills, Ph.D, *Sanity, Insanity and Common Sense: The Groundbreaking New Approach to Happiness* (New York: Ballantine, Fawcett Columbine, 1987.) Out of print.

Chapter Three

Parker, J. Palmer, *A Hidden Wholeness: The Journey Toward and Undivided Life*, Jossey-Bass, A Wiley Imprint, San Francisco, CA 2004, pages 58-59

Chapter Four

Marianne Williamson, *A Return to Love* (New York: Harper Paperbacks, 1992), p. 35

Wayne Dyer, *You'll See It When You Believe It* (New York: William Morrow, 1989)

David R. Hawkins, M.D., Ph.D. *Power VS. Force: The Hidden Determinants of Human Behavior* (Hay House, Inc., Carlsbad, CA 2002) p. 235

Chapter Five

www.thesecret.tv

Chapter Six

Byron Katie, *Loving What Is*, Harmony Books, NY, 2002

Chapter Seven

Lillie's Loose, from the book, *Coming Home*, by Sue Pettit, available from The WV Initiative for Innate Health, Robert C

Byrd Health Sciences Center, 1 Medical Center Drive,
PO Box 9147, Morgantown, WV 26506-9147

Chapter Eight

Wayne Dyer, *Gifts from Eykis* (New York, Pocket Books,
1983), pp. 118-119

Chapter Nine

Valerie Seeman Moreton, N.D., *Heal the Cause* (San Diego:
Kalos Publishing, 1996)

Moreton, p. 64

Moreton, pp. 269-270

Chapter Eleven

Marianne Williamson, *A Return to Love* (New York: Harper
Paperbacks, 1992), p.35

Deepak Chopra, *The Seven Laws of Spiritual Success* (San
Rafael: Amber-Allen Publishing & New World Library, 1994)

Chapter Twelve

Deepak Chopra, *The Seven Laws of Spiritual Success* (San Rafael, CA: Amber-Allen Publishing & New World Library, 1994) pp. 75-76.

Chapter Thirteen

Jefferson Lewis, *Something Hidden: A biography of Wilder Penfiled* (Garden City, New York: Doubleday & Company, Inc., 1981), p. 201

Lewis, p. 198.

Valerie Seeman Moreton, N.D., *Heal the Cause* (San Diego: Kalos Publishing, 1996) p. 339

A Course in Miracles: Workbook for Students (Huntington Station, New York: The Foundation for Inner Peace) p. 8

Ibid p.11

Other Books by Jane Nelsen

Raising Self-Reliant Children in a Self-Indulgent World
H. Stephen Glenn and Jane Nelsen

Parents Who Love Too Much
How Good Parents Can Learn to Love More Wisely and
Develop Children of Character
Jane Nelsen and Cheryl Erwin

Positive Time Out:
Over 50 Ways to Avoid Power Struggles
in Homes and Classrooms
Jane Nelsen

Pup Parenting
Lynn Lott and Jane Nelsen

In the Positive Discipline Series

Positive Discipline
Jane Nelsen

Positive Discipline: The First Three Years
Jane Nelsen, Cheryl Erwin, and Roslyn Duffy

Positive Discipline for Teenagers
Jane Nelsen and Lynn Lott

Positive Discipline A–Z,
Jane Nelsen, Lynn Lott, and H. Stephen Glenn

Positive Discipline in the Classroom,
Jane Nelsen, Lynn Lott, and H. Stephen Glenn

Positive Discipline: A Teacher's A–Z Guide
Jane Nelsen, Roslyn Duffy, Linda Escobar,
Kate Ortolano,
and Debbie Owen-Sohocki

Positive Discipline for Single Parents
Jane Nelsen, Cheryl Erwin, and Carol Delzer

Positive Discipline for Child Care Providers
Jane Nelsen and Cheryl Erwin

Positive Discipline for Working Parents
Jane Nelsen and Lisa Larson

EBOOKS

Positive Discipline for Parenting in Recovery
Jane Nelsen, Lynn Lott, Riki Intner

Positive Discipline for Step Families
Jane Nelsen, Cheryl Erwin, and H. Stephen Glenn

Order information

For printed books please visit
http://www.empoweringpeople.com

For additional information please visit
http://www.positivediscipline.com

For e-books please visit
http://www.focusingonsolutions.com

To order product by phone please call
1-800-456-7770

Jane Nelsen is available for lectures and
workshops. jane@positivediscipline.com

About the Author

Dr. Jane Nelsen is the mother of seven children and grandmother to 19 grandchildren. She is California licensed Marriage, Family and Child Therapist and the author and/or coauthor of eighteen books and two curriculum manuals: Teaching Parenting the Positive Discipline Way and Positive Discipline Workshops. Jane lives with her husband, Barry, in South Jordan, UT and San Clemente, CA